רכב על האפריון
(Riding Upon The Palanquin)

I0356334

An Esoteric Telestic (Qabbalistic) Commentary on the Book of The Apocalypse

BY הרב מג בבל רז אשר עמרקה
[Rab Mag (The Chief Magician) of Mystery Bablyon which is AM-(e)-RIQAH (The People of Rebekkah)]

Acknowledgments

This book took over a year to complete. During this time, I desperately searched and prayed for someone to do the cover art who was a true Holy Initiate and Adept. It took 2 years to find this person. I am proud to now say that this special individual is now one of my chief disciples and a very advanced holy Adept. He prayed and fasted over the cover art which I dictated to him.

The cover art that you now see is his holy work. This image, to my understanding is the most powerful and divine image I truly believe with all my heart and spirit that has ever been done and completed. The image was my own vision which I explained to this holy most skillful artist. It is a very powerful occult supernal image of which again, I truly believe has never been done. The divinity and power of this image has been esoteric for over 2000 years! Now, I reveal it to the world for the first time, the full occult revelation of our Holy Goddess! Those who are of the narrow and straight Way, will know and understand!

Again, I simply cannot emphasize the power and divinity of this image! It simply cannot be fully expressed in words. Only those who belong to our most eternal primordial esoteric Order will be able to fully comprehend. In sooth, it is a holy divine mandela of the highest order. I encourage all to fully meditate on it and open and enter the higher holy gates of יהוה. Amen!

So thank you Francisco Rivera, one of my chief and most beloved Yisraeli disciples for revealing what has been concealed for many Ages! יהוה shall keep and bless thee and thy family for all the eternal aeons!

Exordium

This book is a running Qabbalistic Commentary on the Book of Revelation. Its primary focus is on the esoteric and mystical aspects of the Book. In all, the purpose is to give divine revelation on the Book that has been sealed from both Jew and Goy in general for about 2,000 years.

It should be duly noted that there are certain esoteric topics briefly covered in this Commentary which are not given their proper treatment. For this reason, I first divert my readers to my first Treatise Restoration of the WORD of YHWH. The Treatise should aid the reader in further understanding certain esoteric topics only given minor treatment in this Commentary.

Because this book is a high-level Qabbalistic commentary, this Book is only intended for Israelites who are initiated into the low grades of the Divine Mysteries. As a pre-requisite, the reader is assumed to have a good knowledge and familiarity with the now readily available ancient esoteric Israeli literature viz. Sefer HaZohar and etc.

The Book of the Apocalypse is the most Jewish and Qabbalastic book of the entire WORD! And if you do not know this, then it because you are not a Jew, or you have not been initiated into the Divine Mysteries. Since this book is entirely anagogical and Qabbalastic, I feel it is requisite that I present the most fitting isagoge given by two of the greatest divine Hierophants of ancient wise origin:

"*And in all the other Divine enlightenments which the occult tradition of our inspired teachers hath, by mystic interpretation, accordant with the Scriptures, bestowed upon us, we also have been initiated : apprehending these things in the present life (according to our powers), through the sacred veils of that loving kindness which in the Scriptures and the Hierarchical Traditions, enwrappeth spiritual truths in terms drawn from the world of sense, and super-essential truths in terms drawn from Being, clothing with shapes and forms things which are shapeless and formless, and by a variety of separable symbols, fashioning manifold attributes of the imageless and supernatural Simplicity...But at present we employ (so far as in us lies), appropriate symbols for things Divine; and then from these we press on upwards according to our powers to behold in simple unity the Truth perceived by spiritual contemplations, and leaving behind us all human notions of godlike things, we still the activities of our minds, and reach (so far as this may be) into the Super-Essential Ray, wherein all kinds of knowledge so have their pre-existent limits (in a transcendently inexpressible manner), that we cannot conceive nor utter It, nor in any wise contemplate the same, seeing that It surpasseth all things, and wholly exceeds our knowledge, and super-essentially contains beforehand (all conjoined within Itself) the bounds of all natural sciences and forces (while yet its force is not circumscribed by any), and so possesses, beyond the celestial Intelligences, Its firmly fixed abode. For if all the branches of knowledge belong to things that have being, and if their limits have reference to the existing world, then that which is beyond all Being must also be transcendent above all knowledge.*" (Dionysios the Areopagite: On the Divine Names and Mystical Theology Chapter I 4.).

"*Each also imitates both the intelligible and celestial order of the Gods; and contains the eternal measures of beings, and those admirable signatures which are hither from the Demiurgus and father of wholes, by which things of an ineffable nature are unfolded into light through arcane symbols, things formless are vanquished by forms, thing more excellent than every image are expressed through image, and all things are accomplished through a divine cause alone...*" (Iamblißos On The Mysteries of the Egyptians, Chaldeans, and Assyrians [Section 1 Chapter 22 from the Thomas Taylor Translation]).

Apropos, the time has now arrived, as it is written:

"*...bar the words and seal The Book until the time of consummation until many are taught and knowledge is increased.*" (Theodotion on Sefer Daniyel 12:4)

Indeed, THE 144 have arrived and are here!!!

א

THE BEGINNING

The Gate to the Revelation

There are two sections of The Holy WORD that form the entire foundation and cornerstone of the entire esoteric Qabbalah. The first is:

"*You will proclaim* חכמה *(ĥOĥMAH)…for on the highest tops She is, and between the paths She takes Her stand, for besides the gates of the rulers She takes Her seat, and at the entrances She sings hymns.*" (LXX Hebrew Book of Israeli Proverbs 8:1-3).

Duly note that ĥOĥMAH is emphatically feminized in the chapter! This is to emphasize the truth that ĥOĥMAH here is Lower ĥOĥMAH, the only begotten Divine Daughter, the Daughter of the Holy King. Another proof being that our most ancient known disciples, the Greeks, always equate SOPHIA as the female Deity. Yet our principal text Sefer HaZohar has ĥOĥMAH being principally male as it is written:

"י *is ḫOḫMAH, The Father.*" (Sefer Tiqquney HaZohar 32A).

There is of course no contradiction. This is Upper ḫOḫMAH the supernal root and source of The Daughter in the mystery of Bathuel:

"*'BATHUEL', a name meaning in our speech 'Daughter of God'; yea, a true-born and ever-virgin daughter, who, by reason alike of her own modesty and of the glory of Him that begot her...How pray, can ḫOḫMAH, the Daughter of El, be rightly spoken of as a Father? Is it because, while ḫOḫMAH's name is feminine, her nature is manly?...For that which comes after El, even though it were chiefest of all other things, occupies a second place, and therefore was termed feminine to express it contrast with the Maker of the Universe who is masculine and its affinity to everything else.*" (Philon On Flight and Finding 51).

As it is written:

"*'Through ḫOḫMAH, יהוה founded the Earth...'*" *(Ancient Israeli Book of Proverbs 3:19).*

"*With ḫOḫMAH who is the Father. He founded the Daughter which is the Earth.*" (Sefer Tiqquney HaZohar 61B).

We read:

"*And נחה (NOḫAH) (She shall rest) upon him...*" (11:2).

Who is *She* and *him*? Lo, it is written:

"*And a King shall come forth...HaMashiaḫ...and there shall rest upon him the spirit of....*" (Targum Ibid.).

Hence, *him* refers to HaMashiaḫ. *She*, then, evidently refers to his Mother SHEḫINAH or NOḫAH who is one with Her husband who is:

"*...נח (NOAḫ) The Man who is TZADDIQ...*" (Sefer Breyshith 6:9).

TZADDIQ representing the Divine Phallus inside The Divine Pudendum who is SHEɧINAH. She, along with Him, are enclothed by the 7 Emanations above them which are:

"*...the spirit of* יהוה*, the spirit of ɧOɧMAH and BINAH, the spirit of EYTZAH and GEBURAH, the spirit of DAATH and of the YIRAH of* יהוה." (Sefer Yeshayahu 11:2).

Thus, there are a total of 9 emanations if we include the bottom one, SHEɧINAH, as 2. This is valid since HaMashiaɧ is the son of TZADDIQ, made in his image, so through him, we may add one extra to the count. Now, it must be remembered that according to the ancient esoteric mathematical principles (Im HaKollel [with the sum]) of Gematria:

$x = x+1$; where x is a numeric variable.

This, of course, is a basis of the Golden Ratio[1] known long ago before the goyim rediscovered it; but this is a proof for another time. Ergo, 9=10, which is the secret of the word אלהים (Alohim) which becomes:

הם י אל (They The 10 are God).

As it is veraciously written:

"*10 Sfiroth of Nothingness; 10 and NOT 9! 10 and NOT 11!*" (Sefer Yetzirah 1:4).

"הבן בחכמה *(Understand with ɧOɧMAH). Be wise with Understanding. Examine with them and probe them. Make* דבר *(The WORD) stand on its essence and make the Creator sit on his base.*" (Ibid.).

[1] The Mathematical Golden Ratio is $x^2 = x+1$. Thus, Im Kollel is one dimension lower, residing in the paradoxical world of the Supernatural where antinomies abound as Truths such as 1 = 0! Highly Initiated Occult Mathematicians such as myself will know and understand.

Finally, we have the Daughter NOɧAH. Again, one arrives at a total of 9 emanations. But one must not forget that the entire Sfiroth acts as one emanation through Im HaKollel. Ergo, the Holy Divine Decad. And so I have correctly restored the order and enumeration of HaSfiroth after the secret behind the order of the Tetragrammaton. י representing the Father. First ה representing the Mother. ו representing the six sons as ONE since this Hebrew letter has a Gematria of 6; mystery of:

"*...the sons of my mother were angry with me...*" (Shir HaShirim 1:6).

The proof being that the letter ו (*waw)* fully spelled out is equal to '*one*' fully spelled out in Hebrew:

ואו (waw) = 13 = אחד (One).

And second ה representing the Daughter. Hence, the secret behind the Tetragrammaton is correctly and holistically understood by Qabbalists.

The Divine Revelation given to me by HASARAH HASHAMAYIM BATHUEL (The Princess of The Heavens The Daughter of God aka The Holy Spiritess):

1:3 ~ "Blessed is he that readeth, and they that hear the words of this prophecy, and keep those things which are written therein: for the time is at hand."

Verily, I say unto ye my dear readers, INDEED THE TIME IS AT HAND!!! Literally, we are in the time!!! It is as it is written:

"*For nation shall rise against nation, and kingdom against kingdom: and there shall be famines, and pestilences, and earthquakes, in divers places.*" (Sefer Mattityahu 24:7).

"*At that time, wars will be aroused in the war – nation against nation, city against city, and countless new afflictions will come upon Yisrael...*" (Sefer HaZohar ḫadash 6d).

Those that *have eyes to see and ears to hear* will more than understand!

1:4 ~ "...the seven Spirits which are before his Throne."

Lo, it is written:

"*ḫOḫMAH built herself a HOUSE and supported it with Seven Pillars*." (Book of Proverbs 9:1).

Yet, the verse supra is in reference to Upper ḫOḫMAH. As above so below, hence we must not forget about Lower ḫOḫMAH as it is written:

"בראשית *(With BEGINNING)*..." (Sefer Breyshith 1:1)

Do not read בראשית but ב ראשית (2 BEGINNING), that is, there are 2 *BEGINNINGS* as is perfectly explained in HaSefer HaZohar:

"*Thus, 'By ḫOḫMAH a house is built' [Book of Proverbs 24:3]...the upper HOUSE is built by ḫOḫMAH and the lower one as well...The secret is:* ב ראשית בראשית *2 BEGINNING...*" (1:29b).

And what is *BEGINNING*? As it is written:

"*With ḫOḫMAH* ..." (Targum Yerushalmi on Sefer Breyshith 1:1)

As it is written:

"ראשית חכמה" (*BEGINNING* is *ḫOḫMAH*)" (Sefer Tehillim 111:10).

Another veracious interpretation being:

ב ראשית (2 is BEGINNING or ḫOḫMAH) that is: ḫOḫMAH is the 2nd Emanation.

And there are 8 Emanations below Upper ḫOḫMAH including Her House. As above so below as it is written:

"*There are 7 pillars upon which the world stands.*

'...7 and 7...' (Sefer Zeḫaryahu 4:2).

7 established below corresponding to those above...7 upper ones and 7 lower ones, conjoined as one." (Sefer HaZohar ḫadash 62B).

Ergo, there are 7 spirits or divine entities below The HOUSE which are the 7 Archons or Archangels. They are in the image of the Lower 7 Sfiroth. Thus, it follows that this Throne spoken of here must at the very least be Lower ḫOḫMAH since the next verse ties Yeshua HaMashiaḫ to this verse who is tied and connected to Lower ḫOḫMAH as will be explained later in more detail with the aid of my Holy Rock.

1:6 ~ "And hath made us kings and kohanim unto El and his Father"

This verse is a very great mystery that the goyim do not understand! These are Israelites! Royalty and priesthood are always and only retained in The Family, in this case The Royal Spiritual Family of YHWH, as is written to us Israelites:

"*Ye are sons of* יהוה*...*" (Sefer Debarim 14:1).

This is not so for the other goyim as it is written:

"*He sheweth his WORD unto YAQOB, his statutes and his judgments unto Israel.*
He hath not dealt so with any goy: and as for his judgments, they have not known them. Halleluyah." (Sefer Tehillim 147:19-20).

This is all an established fact of the Holy Divine Word!!! The wise and shining intelligent ones will know and understand.

1:8 ~ "I am א(ALEF) and ת(TAW), ראשית (BEGINNING) and the ENDING, saith הויה יהוה (which is), ויהוה (which was), והיה (and which is to come)..."

As it is written:

"*Hear me O Yaqob and Yisrael, whom I call, I AM THE FIRST (BEGINNING) and I AM THE END.*" (Sefer Yeshayahu 48:13).

Now, את, being polysemous, like every Hebrew word, has several meanings (7 to be exact) in ancient Hebrew. The first is the accusative particle while another is the second person feminine pronoun (*you*). Ergo, the reason why את is known as NOђAH (REST) or the lower female deity among modern Jewish Qabbalists and stated en passim in HaSefer HaZohar. But, technically, this requires further attention! For example, HaSefer HaZohar states:

"...את־השמים *(the Heavens) – VOICE and mate...*" (1:15b)

So, HaSefer HaZohar will have you believe that the Heavens are YESOD, and that את, or NOђAH, is his mate. However, this is technically not precise! In fact, these words in the Hebrew Torah constitute an equation through the Mappiq (־)! That is, את is *the Heavens* which is YESOD. Ergo, את is masculine NOT feminine! The proof is as it is written by one of the most initiated Saints:

"*And **HE** said unto me, It is done. I am* א *and* ת*...*" (Book of Apocalypse 21:6).

The proof that את refers to the masculine TZADDIQ is:

"*And He was called* את ־ שמו *(*את *is his name) who is NOAђ...*" (Sefer Breyshith 5:29).

Again, the mappiq (־) equates את with his name. Ergo, through transitive relation, את is NOAђ who is TZADDIQ. Additionally:

"*Honor* את ־ אביך *(thy Father)* ואת ־ אמך *(thy Mother)...*" (Sefer Shmoth 20:12).

Which mirrors:

"...את־השמים *(the Heavens)* ואת ־ הארץ *(the Earth).*" (Sefer Breyshith 1:1).

Ergo, it is proven that את refers to the male Sfirah. As such, this would make אתה, the second person masculine pronoun (*you*), represent NOȟAH; which makes perfect sense considering the feminine suffix ה. And through Im Kollel, אתה (Gematria of 406) is equivalent to ואת (Gematria of 407). And it should be readily clear why ואת is feminine from the verses supra. This is the path of truth.

And this leads to an even greater mystery or enigma. How can את represent the masculine deity when the word signifies a feminine pronoun and vice versa??? Sefer HaZohar knowing this exactly, asks the same question, hinting at the underlying error for the truly initiated!

"*If you say את is always female – come and see.* ת *is female,* א *is male – fused together as one! Then the female is seen in fullness, comprised in the mystery of all letters. Thus, even though* ת *is female, it is encompassed within the sphere of the male.*" (Zohar ȟadash [Shir HaShirim] 66b).

This requires further explication. This is a high-level paradox pertaining to the Spirit Realm. Remember, that Realm is not governed by the laws of our physical universe. From our vantage point, it is rife with paradoxes and antinomies! Nevertheless, this enigma is to teach us a sublime truth. Anent the shapeshifting and holographic aspect of the Godhead, Sefer HaZohar states:

"*This Angel (referring to Lower ȟOȟMAH) is sometimes male and sometimes female. When providing blessing it is male...And when it stands in judgment over the world, it is called female...Correspondingly it is written: 'flame of the whirling SWORD' (Gen.3:24).*" (1:232a)

As it is written:

"*Whirling-changing: sometimes male, sometimes female...*" (Breyshith Rabba 21:9).

This divine mystery is best explained by the ancient Hierophant:

"*'BATHUEL', a name meaning in our speech 'Daughter of God'; yea, a true-born and ever-virgin daughter, who, by reason alike of her own modesty and of the glory of Him that begot her...How pray, can ɧOɧMAH, the Daughter of El, be rightly spoken of as a Father? Is it because, while ɧOɧMAH's name is feminine, her nature is manly?...For that which comes after El, even though it were chiefest of all other things, occupies a second place, and therefore was termed feminine to express it contrast with the Maker of the Universe who is masculine and its affinity to everything else.*" (Philon On Flight and Finding 51).

And yet, I do not find this divine Hierophant's answer to his own question satisfactory. For it was one day that a divine voice within me exclaimed the root of the holy mystery:

BATHUEL is The Daughter of EL or the Holy Divine Daughter. But She is also The Holy Divine Father as it is written:

"*Bathuel thy Mother's Father...*" (Sefer Breyshith 22:23).

And She is also The Holy Divine Son as it is written:

"*Bathuel the Son of The Queen...*" (Sefer Breyshith 24:24).

Holy Mystery of the many aspects of The Holy Divine Trinity. And so it is, Alohim is both male and female as ONE. As the mystery of the Tetragrammaton reveals read backwards:

הי (She) הו (He) or HE-SHE

Indeed, a hermaphrodite entity. As it is written:

"*And Alohim (The Gods) made ADAM, according to the image of Alohim he made him, Male and Female he created them.*" (Sefer Breyshith 1:27).

Here, we have the actual, albeit esoteric, description of Alohim. Take note that Adam is made in the image of Alohim. This image, as explicitly stated, is both male and female as One. Ergo, or equivalently, the archetype, Alohim, MUST also be both male and female as one!!! Ergo, the proof of the feminine deity in the Godhead. Interestingly, we find this proof and allusion of the nature and quintessence of Alohim in the 26th verse in the ancient Hebrew Massorah, the exact Gematria of the Tetragrammaton!

And so את represents TZADDIQ or the 9th emanation. So in the lower Godhead he represents the male, the divine archetypal phallus. But when one with his mate NOꞕAH, with respect to the rest of the entire Godhead, he is seen as feminine being subject to the Upper Godhead/Sfiroth. Yes, the wise and brilliant intelligent one will know and understand.

Now, this has to be all said because Sefer HaZohar, en passim, equates both את and אתה with NOꞕAH! As already proven, this requires further attention. One is masculine the other feminine with respect to the Lower Godhead. Moreover, on a supernatural level they are interchangeable. Nevertheless, both are ONE. And the root and foundation is את, which as just shown may symbolize the totality of Lower ꞕOꞕMAH or either NOꞕAH or TZADDIQ which are ONE. Ergo, we may also perceive Lower ꞕOꞕMAH as a shapeshifting hermaphroditic entity. This is more approximate to the Supernal Truth.

Now, The FIRST not only alludes to Lower ꞕOꞕMAH as just explicated who is the beginning of the Lower Worlds. It also alludes to Upper ꞕOꞕMAH who is the beginning of the Upper Worlds as is well explained:

"*This is the meaning of 'I am FIRST' – It is the mystery of the spreading of Emanation from above to below. And 'I am LAST' is the existence of the reflecting light that goes back from below to above. This is the meaning of 'FIRST' and 'LAST'. KETHER is called The FIRST...*" (Rab Mushah Qordovero Pardes Rimonim Gate 3 Chapter 1).

And so one sees how the phrase alludes to all of HaSfiroth from Upper ḫOḫMAH, which includes Upper KETHER, to Lower ḫOḫMAH, which includes Lower KETHER.

Take note of one of the ancient Qabbalastic invocations of blessing which contains three permutations or anagrams of the Sacred Tetragrammaton; representing the Holy Trinity.

1:12-14 ~ "And I turned to see the voice that spake with me. And being turned, I saw seven golden candlesticks; And in the midst of the seven candlesticks one like unto the Son of Man...and girt about the paps with a golden girdle. His head and his hairs were white like wool, as white as snow; and his eyes were as a flame of fire."

Now, one would be tempted to state and believe that this likeness of the Son of Man is YESHUAH HaMashiaḫ. But, this is not the case! Unfortunately, many ignorant goyim who are not Jewish and well acquainted with our ancient esoteric doctrines just don't know any better. But, it is understandable, as will soon become apparent.

So who is the likeness of this Son of Man mentioned here? HaAlohim (The GODS) or the full DECAD!!! Let us begin with the proof, shall we? We must begin from the beginning, literally.

The Image or Son of HaAlohim, or the Holy Decad/Sfiroth, is called HaAdam (The Man) as it is written:

"*[Yeshua HaMashiaḫ]... Who is the IMAGE of the invisible Alohim,* ***the firstborn of every creature****: For by him were all things created, that are in Heaven, and that are in Earth, visible and invisible...* ***And he is before all things, and by him all things consist****...who is REYSHITH (BEGINNING)...*" (1st Letter to the Colossians 1:14-18).

Ergo, herein lies the momentous equation, namely that ADAM = HaMashiah = The Image of HaAlohim! Ergo, the archetype, HaAlohim or HaSfiroth, must be some likeness of HaAdam! Ergo, in the verse supra, it is the Archetype, in this case the Holy Decad, that is being compared to the Image, specifically *The Son of Man*. Ergo, the reason why we Jewish Qabbalists depict the Godhead symbolically as a Man or HAADAM. In one of the most esoteric folios of HaSefer HaZohar, the Idra Rabba, we have a detailed description of the Godhead as HAADAM or a Man. Likewise, Yoђanan and Daniyel give us a very short summarized description.

The verse above is similar to the vision of the prophet Zeђaryahu as it is written but Qabbalistically read:

"*...behold: a golden Menorah,* כלה *(the Bride) and* גלה *(The Torch [or The Revealed One]) over Her head and 7 candlesticks above Him...*" (Sefer Zeђaryahu 4:2).

And it is also written:

"*...And The Queen stands to the Right in the gold woven clothing decked out in many colors.*" (LXX Sefer Tehillim 45:9).

The Queen is the Divine Upper Mother or ђOђMAH in the Godhead who is symbolized by gold. Hence the reason for the golden Menorah which emerged from Her. The many colors represent the various Sfiroth and their various attributes that emerge from Her. Ergo, the 7 seven candlesticks of the Menorah symbolize the lower 7 Emanations as it is written:

"*ђOђMAH built Herself a HOUSE and supported it with Seven Pillars.*" (Book of Proverbs 9:1).

Now, take careful note that the verses supra begin with singularity, that is, a single voice. That singularity then becomes plurality with the 7 golden candlesticks. Very interestingly, one finds this exact description of this likeness of *The Son of Man* in Sefer Daniyel:

"*...ATTIQ YOMAYA (The ANCIENT of The DAYS) sat..the hair of his head was like pure wool...*" (Sefer Daniyel 7:9).

"*...there was one Man...girded by fine gold...and his body like Tarshish...his eyes like torches of fire...feet like the appearance of gleaming brass, and the sound of his voice like the sound of multitude.*" (Ibid. 10:5-6).

As such, then, the head, being white like pure wool represents ATTIQ YOMAYA or Upper ḫOḫMAH. Next is the body in the secret of תרשיש (Tarshish) which when permuted becomes:

שש (6) יתר (The Faithful)

As in:

"יתר *(Faithful) lips becomes not a fool...*" (Hebrew Book of Israeli Proverbs 17:7).

And *The Faithful 6* or ו is The Son of יה (YAH) as it is written:

"...ו *(Gematria of 6) who is The Son of YAH.*" (Sefer Tiqquney HaZohar 14B).

And the description descends to YAM SOF (The End Sea or Weedy Sea [Red Sea in LXX]) which is made of brass (The SEA (laver) in the Temple Courtyard) and is the 10th emanation represented by 10 toes. For the brass SEA in the Tabernacle is a symbol for SHEḫINAH. Again, in Sefer Daniyel, Daniyel begins the description with singularity through the likeness of a Son of Man, but ends with plurality through the *voices of a multitude.* This is an obvious reference to the seven voices of Alohim, heard on Mount SINAI by our ancestors. And although they are seven, yet they are ONE as it is written in the Psalm of ḫannah, mother of the great Prophet Shamuel:

"*...the barren hathe borne seven...*" (Sefer Shamuel Alef 2:5).

And the most sagacious Israeli Rab of Antiquity, Philon writes:

"*And yet it is the mother of one child-Shamuel-who is speaking. How then can she say that she has borne seven? It can only be in accordance with the truth of things, she holds the ONE to be the same as the SEVEN…*" (The Unchangeableness of God 11).

Another secret. Duly note that The Son of Man is seen in the midst of the 7 candlesticks. Ergo, he is the middle candlestick or The MIDDLE PILLAR. And this is in perfect accordance with our esoteric tradition:

"*The MIDDLE PILLAR is in the likeness of The Son of Man.*" (Sefer HaZohar 2:169B).

Also known as The Son of YAH as it is also written:

"*The Middle Pillar is The Son of YAH.*" (Sefer HaZohar Raaya Mehemna 2:115A).

Amen.

Now, I know many people who have claimed to have visions and have seen YESHUAH Mashiaḫ. But never, not once, have I ever heard descriptions match those of Daniyel and Yoḫanan. That is that they saw him with white hair and fiery eyes, and etc. Why? Because these ancient Israeli Saints were the last of their kind and order! Well, almost. There is a new presently esoteric breed in this last generation. I of course speak of the Chief 144 who are now here; present.

1:15 ~ "And his feet like unto χαλκο-λιβάνῳ (fine white brass), as if they burned in a furnace…"

This is an interesting verse. The Greek word there is a compound word. Χαλκο is the Greek word for fine brass. Fine brass, fully refined in the furnace for purity, is a bright yellow color similar to gold. Hence, why it has always been a cheap substitute for gold. λιβάνῳ is the Greek transliteration for Hebrew word Lebanah, which signifies the color white. Thus, here our Supernal Father and Lord's skin is given a color that is an admixture of gold and white, very similar to the olive skin complexion of us Jews and middle-eastern people. Duly note this color is not the black or brown of the cursed ɧamitic or African race. For Yisrael, was the nephew of Laban (a white man), and not Kush (a black man), kin to the cursed races of the Egyptians and Kaananites!

As stated above, the feet of the Sfiroth or Godhead represent the bottom of the Holy Decad. Since there are 10 feet, they represent the 10th Emanation which is SHEɧINAH as stated above. Duly note that they are brass since THE SEA, another codeword for SHEɧINAH, in the Tabernacle was made of brass.

1:16 ~ "And he had in his right hand seven stars: and out of his mouth went a sharp two-edged SWORD: and his countenance was as the SUN shineth in his strength."

There are a lot of esoteric mystical symbols give here! There is a Right above and below. Here, it most likely signifies the Highest Right which is ɧOɧMAH as it is written:

"*...And The Queen stands to the Right in the gold woven clothing decked out in many colors.*" (LXX Sefer Tehillim 45:9).

Moreover, the *7 stars* are followed by The MOUTH. Thus, the 7 stars would represent the lower 7 Sfiroth because The MOUTH (The Divine Pudendum) is SHEɧINAH as it is written:

"*MALɧUTH is The MOUTH.*" (Sefer Tiqquney HaZohar 17A Pataɧ Eliyahu Prayer).

The sharp two-edged sword represents the 2 ɧerubim. They symbolically represent the 2 first chief sons of SHEɧINAH or RAɧEL vis-à-vis Yosef and Benyamin. They guard the Holy Divine GARDEN who is SHEɧINAH. About them, it is written:

"*Two young children[2], youths, fire-flashing sword-blade in their hands – guarding paths and byways, so that none may enter or*

---

[2] In Aramaic, the Hebrew *ɧerubim* may signify *like a child.*

exit...they were created before this world." (Sefer HaZohar ɧadash Matnitin 3A).

"*SHEɧINAH includes by this 2 ɧerubim – Metatron and Sandalfon.*" (Sefer HaZohar Raaya Mehemna).

This is the secret of:

"*...The EARTH brought forth The Soul – The Living One (or The Living Soul)...*" (Sefer Breyshith 1:24).

On one level, there are 2, the Soul – Sandalfon, and The Living One who is Metatron. On the prime level, however, this is the very first divine entity, the first *living soul*, brought forth by HaAlohim or HaSfiroth; specifically, SHEɧINAH who is The EARTH. This *Living Soul* is Adam Qadmon (Primordial) as it is written:

"*...and Adam became The Living Soul.*" (Ibid. 2:7).

Who is this Primordial Adam or Living Soul? Lo, it is written:

"*[Yeshua HaMashiaɧ]... Who is the IMAGE of the invisible Alohim,* ***the firstborn of every creature****: For by him were all things created, that are in Heaven, and that are in Earth, visible and invisible...* ***And he is before all things, and by him all things consist****...who is REYSHITH (BEGINNING)...*" (1st Letter to the Colossians 1:14-18).

Ergo, the equation between Adam, The First Living Soul, and HaMashiaɧ as has been previously revealed. And who is Metatron? Lo, it is written:

"*When it is said*

'Abraham said to His servant...' (Sefer Breyshith 24:2)

That is the servant of the Omnipresent. The oldest of His house to serve Him. And who is he? That is Metatron...This is as it is written:

'And Abraham said to his servant' (Ibid.)

Namely to Metatron the servant of the Omnipresent. ***The oldest of His house because he Metatron is the first of the creatures of the Omnipresent*** *who rules over all that belongs to Him For the Holy Blessed be He* ***has given him dominion over all His Hosts***" (Sefer HaZohar The Concealed Midrash 1:126b).

Exactly, as one of our most initiated Israelite Rabbanan tells us:

"*To his WORD, his ἀρχάγγελ (First Angel), highest in age...*" (Philon Who is the Heir 205).

And if there is any question as to who is the WORD, then listen to him again:

"*But if there be any as yet unfit to be called a Son of God, let him press to take his place under God's First-born, the WORD, who holds the eldership among the angels, their ruler as it were.*" (Ibid. Confusion of Tongues 146).

Precisely as it is written:

"*...MIߐAEL* אחד*(first) of The Princes/Angels...*" (Sefer Daniyel 10:13).

"*...MIߐAEL the ἀρχάγγελος (First Angel)...*" (Sefer Yehudah 1:9).

Which is why we read:

"*The second exile/revelation is Metatron. He rules and is Viceroy to The King. And next to the Queen sits the Viceroy.*" (Sefer Tiqquney HaZohar Tiqqun 7 14B).

"*Because Metatron is second to The King.*" (Ibid. 15A).
Ergo, the equation between Metatron, Miߐael, and Yeshuah should be readily evident. He is the Prince of The Faces/Presence (specifically the 10 Faces of HaAlohim) as it is written in one our most ancient prayers for Rosh HaShanah in the sections of the Shofar blasts:

“*May it be your will from thy presence that the sounding of the Shofar that we blow be woven in to the curtain by the hand of the Minister Tartiel like the name that was received by the hand of Eliyahu (his memory be for a blessing) and* ***YESHUA The Prince of the Faces and The Prince Metatron****. And may you be filled with mercy for us. Blessed are you Master of Mercies.*” (Maḫzor Rosh Hashanah).

And so we must understand that HaMashiaḫ goes by many titles and names, some exoteric and others esoteric like Metatron. One of his very crucial titles is linked to his essence as a Portal. It is HaShaar or ‘The Gate’ in Hebrew. This is as it is written in our most ancient principal esoteric holy text:

“*This is SHADDAI [which = Metatron in Gematria] who is outside the Mezuzah. But ‘and my Name is* יהוה*’ is inside the Mezuzah which is the gate of The Holy One Blessed Be He. Concerning it, it is said:*

‘This is The Gate of יהוה *...’ [Sefer Tehillim 118:20].*

‘...I was not known to them.’ [Sefer Shmoth 6:3].’” (Sefer Tiqquney HaZohar Tiqqun 22 66A).

Indeed, he, Metatron, Yeshuah HaMashiaḫ *was not know to them*, the Jews! Only the elite most initiated of Jews like myself! And so this is why it is also written:

“*I am The Gate. If anyone enters in by me, he will be saved...*” (Sefer Yoḫanan 10:9).

Indeed, he is משיח (Mashiaḫ) or משח (from The THOUGHT), that is from the Divine Lower THOUGHT; namely Lower ḫOḫMAH! Amen, amen, as should be readily apprehended, He, The Blessed Holy One, goes by many esoteric theurgic names or titles such as ḫOḫMAH, YAHUEL, and etc.

The First or Chief Archon from HaSfiroth is Metatron or HaMashiaḫ. His countenance is likened to the SUN, his Father who is The MIDDLE PILLAR as it is written:

"*Illumination glistening yellow all around like the SUN. This is TIFERETH.*" (Sefer Tiqquney HaZohar 1A).

"*And Metatron is in the likeness of TZADDIQ.*" (Ibid. 4A).

And TZADDIQ is also in The MIDDLE PILLAR. And marvel not that the SUN stands for The Son of YAH for an ancient divine Initiator wrote:

"*...the Sun, in accordance with the rules of allegory is likened to the ruler and Father of*
The Universe." (Philon On Dreams I 73).

"*The third meaning in which he employs the title 'Sun' is that of The Logos (Divine Word).*" (Philon On Dreams I85).

This is because, according to the ancients, and veraciously so, The Sun is in the 4th Sphere, being in the middle of the 7 Heavenly Spheres as it is written:

"*For the Sun, like the candlestick, has the 4th place in the middle of the six...*" (Philo Judaeus Moses II 103).

Ergo, The first meaning is TIFERETH. The second is YESOD or TZADDIQ who is also in in The Middle Pillar. Ergo, the 3rd represents Metatron or HaMashiaḫ. But, remember, he is likened to the SUN, because he is made in the image of The SUN who is YESOD through TIFERETH since YAQOB, Lower ḫOḫMAH is his Father. And it is like the Son to take on the seal and appellations of his Father. For just as his Father, TZADDIQ has 12 Divine Elders below Him, so too Yeshuah had 12 disciples below him.

It is now very critical and momentous to understand the way of mystical truth. The Divine Son must not be confused! There is the Divine Son within The Holy Decad or HaSfiroth who is known as ו.

This represents the lower 6 Emanations or Sons as ONE as stated in Introduction. The Middle Pillar or Tifereth, who represents the entirety, is also known as The Son of YAH. And TZADDIQ who is in his image also represents The Son of YAH. But all together, the entire 6 are one! This is the Divine Son within the Godhead. Metatron or HaMashiaḫ is the firstborn son outside the Godhead or HaSfiroth. Ergo, he is known as The Son of HaAlohim or the Godhead. He is made in the image of The Divine Son within the Godhead. Hence, the reason for all the confusion and perplexment among all modern day Jews and Qabbalists. Now, the truth has been clearly explicated and illuminated.

Continuing on the telestic equation between Metatron/Yeshuah and The Son within the Godhead; a few additional points. The letter צ (Tzadi) is equated or associated with the Hebrew word Tzaddiq (the righteous one), a symbol for the 9th Emanation who is TZADDIQ or Lower ḫOḫMAH. Lo, it is written:

"*Why does צ have 2 forms? This is [in reference] to Mashiaḫ*" (Othiyoth (Letters of) d'Rab Aqiba)

Ergo, it is evident that the letter צ is equated with righteousness and Mashiaḫ. Lo, there is another variant manuscript of the above text that reads

"*Why does צ have 2 heads? Because it is Yeshua of Natzoreth…who stood and led people astray…*" (Ibid.).

Hmmm. Yes, the Most High Initiate will know and understand the secret and mystery!

Another interpretation linked to the previous one given:

"*The head of the Sword is י. The body of the Sword is ו. Its double-edgeness is הה. It's sheath is ADONAY (another version: and the sword of יהוה). And when יהוה is outside of His SHEḫINAH, She is judgment that cuts on all sides. When She enters the Sheath She becomes mercies and does not decree judgments. And the secret of the Sword is in its sheath.* יאהדונהי *certainly.*" (Sefer Tiqquney HaZohar 44B).

And it is Metatron, The Lower Sword who is in the image of The Upper Sword. The High Initiate will know and understand.

1:18 ~ "I am he that liveth, and was dead…"

This is an obvious reference to HaMashiaɧ or Lower ɧOɧMAH. Yoɧanan's afflatus and interactions with the Godhead simultaneously switch in and out of plurality and singularity. One moment, Upper ɧOɧMAH, another Lower ɧOɧMAH. Yet, all at the same time. The Epopt will know and understand.

1:18 ~ "The mystery of the seven stars which thou sawest in my right hand, and the seven golden candlesticks. The seven stars are the angels of the seven synagogues: and the seven candlesticks which thou sawest are the seven synagogues."

Mystery of the Mystery: The 7 stars are the lower 7 Emanations and the 7 synagogues are the 7 Great Heyɧaloth (Palaces) or Levels of Heaven. Of these, it is written:

"*There are 7 Palaces – Abodes – above, which are mystery of supernal faith, and there are 7 Palaces below matching them, one corresponding to the other.*" (Sefer HaZohar 1:38A).

Sefer HaZohar goes on to describe them in more detail. Each of the 7 Emanations is the chief Governor of his Palace. Mystery of the matter, essence of the matter: each Emanation is a Palace! The highly Initiated will know and understand.

2:10 ~ "…ye shall have tribulation ten days…"

Mystery of the 10 Plagues. One for each Divine Degree.

2:12-13 ~ "..to the church in Pergamos…where is the seat of HaSatan and where HaSatan dwelleth."

We know from the ancient standing temples, the one in this city was of Zeus and his altar. The same one that was brought to Germany in the early 20th century and caused World War II! Now here is revelation. Baal, the false El spoken of in HaTorah is none other than what the Greeks call Zeus! Proof is found in the ancient veracious historical records. Flavius Josephus, one of the most initiated Israelites and kohanim (priests), writes:

"*This Baal was the God of the Tyrians…*" (Jewish Antiquities Book 9 138).

And he also cites a famous Greek translation of a very ancient Phoenician text that records the history of King ɧiram of Tzor (Tyre):

"*…his son Eiromos(King ɧiram)…set up the golden column in the temple Zeus.*" (Ibid. Book 8 144).

Thus, it is an established fact to any true Biblical Scholar that we have one momentous equation here:

HaSatan = Zeus = Baal. Q.E.D.

And no marvel, for it is written:

"*…I beheld HaSatan as lightening fall from heaven.*" (Book of Luke 10:18).

And this fits the ancient descriptions of Zeus. In Homer's Iliad, Zeus is referred to as the God of Lightening, God of the Sky, and the Cloud Gatherer. This is very interesting, because these are ancient titles given to HaSatan. For example, the high-level Qabbalist and Apostle Shaul writes:

"*Wherein in time past ye walked according to the Aeon (Emanation) of this world, according to the Prince of the Power of the Air, the spirit that now worketh in the children of disobedience.*" (Letter to the Ephesians 2:2).

Divine Revelation: In very ancient Hebrew, HaSatan was known under the title Baal Shaḫjaq (Lord of the Sky/Air). The Hebrew word שחק (Shaḫjaq) can signify sky, clouds, or air. In Aramaic, he is known as Bel Awir (Lord of the Air). And among modern Satanists and Black Magicians as Bel Air, incidentally an evil city in the state of California inhabited predominantly by wealthy and powerful Satanists. Prophetically speaking, soon this city will be utterly destroyed like Sodom and Gomorah. Amen.

2:17 ~ "…To him that overcometh will I give to eat of the hidden man and will give him a white stone, and in the stone a new name written, which no man knoweth saving he that receiveth it."

This is a very great mystery and represents one of the highest arcanum. Lo! It is written:

"*I have said, Ye are Alohim; and all of you are sons of the most High.*" (Sefer Tehillim 82:6).

As stated previously, being called *sons of* יהוה in HaTorah, that signifies that we are in the Royal Spiritual Family of Alohim. As such, that means we are a species of the *summum genus* Alohim or God. Ergo, the reason we are called Alohim!!! And what can be better than becoming Alohim and being Alohim!!! As it is written:

"*For since the beginning of the Aeon they have not heard, nor perceived by the ear, neither hath the eye seen, O Alohim, beside thee, what he hath prepared for him that waiteth for him.*" (Sefer Yeshayahu 64:4).

Yes, Indeed.

Additional proof, of course, is the white stone given to us. Only we Qabbalists know about this white stone. Anent the description of Alohim, we read in HaTorah:

"*And they saw Elohey Yisrael: and there was under his feet as it were a paved work* לבנת*(tiled/bricked) sapphire stone...*" (Sefer Shmoth 24:10).

The Hebrew word לבנת can also signify the color white. Now read the text as we Qabbalists have always esoterically read it:

"*And they saw Elohey Yisrael: and there was under his feet as it were a paved work of crystal diamond (white sapphire/precious stone) ...*" (Sefer Shmoth 24:10).

And so now, we have identified the mysterious white precious gemstone that has always alluded and escaped the goyim. So now, ye shall readily comprehend what Alohim signifies when he tells his afflicted holy saints:

"*O thou afflicted, and unsteady, and not comforted, behold, I will lay thy stones with fair colours, and lay thy foundations with sapphires.*" (Sefer Yeshayahu 54:11).

Precisely and Exactly. We will become like Him. Just as his foundation is overlaid with sapphires, so will ours! The true distinguishing mark of a real El.

Who is the hidden man? Back to our holy ancient principal text which illuminates the hidden:

"*Of this is written:*

'Look, I am about to rain down for you bread from the HEAVENS.' [Sefer Shmoth 16:4].

- *from the HEAVENS, surely!...In the Book of Rab Yeiba he said as follows:*

'...they gathered double bread...' [Sefer Shmoth 16:22].

What does double mean? Two breads. Bread from HEAVEN and bread from EARTH – one a pastry; one a bread of poverty...so bread joins with bread, becoming double." (Sefer HaZohar 1:246a).

Thus, equating bread with Lower ჩOჩMAH. Specifically, a byproduct of The HEAVENS. This is Metatron or The WORD who is from The HEAVENS. The EARTH, the female, symbolizing matzah (unleavened bread) through his soulmate. And our most ancient Israeli hierophant, a Baal of this ancient holy text is in full accord:

"*When they saw what it is that nourished the soul for as Mushah says:*

'..they knew not what it was...' [Sefer Shmoth 16:15].

They became learners and found it to be a LOGON (SAYING or WORD) of Alohim, that is the LOGOS (WORD) of Alohim, from which all kinds of instruction and wisdom flow in perpetual stream." (Philon On Flight and Finding 137).

Ergo, the WORD, the male aspect of Lower ჩOჩMAH is the *hidden man* of the HEAVENS as it is She, Lower ჩOჩMAH, who stated:

"*Come, eat of my bread, and drink of the wine which I have mingled for you.*" (Book of Proverbs 9:5).

And it indeed it was the image or Son of Lower ჩOჩMAH, the humble Architect of the tribe of Yehudah or the Universe that said:

"*...Yeshua took bread, and blessed, and brake it, and gave to them, and said,* ***Take, eat: this is my body****. And he took the cup...And he said unto them,* ***This is my blood of the new testament****, which is shed for many.*" (Book of Mark 14:22-24).

And yet, this all goes back to the hidden meaning of the

Hebrew word *man*. For it signifies '*from NUN (The ETERNAL with a Gematria of 50)*', who is BINAH, and the 50 supernal Portals of our Heavenly Mother! And it is obvious that Her Son is from Her holy Matrix.

But the easiest and most obvious proof is that great Teaching in our divine legislation:

"*For Adam shall not live by bread alone but by every WORD that proceeds from the mouth of Alohim shall he live.*" (LXX Sefer Debarim 8:3).

Ergo, it simply and logically follows that the WORD is the bread of HaAlohim or *man*.

It is only the true pure-blooded Jews who have eyes and ears to contemplate, see, hear, and understand all these mysteries.

2:28 ~ "...And I will give him the MORNING STAR."

This morning star is YESHUAH HaMashiaḫ, as it is written:

"*I YESHUAH...am the bright and MORNING STAR.*" (Book of Apocalypse 22:16).

"*To the chief Musician, upon the* אילת השחר *(The MORNING GODDESS/STARESS)...they pierced my hands and my feet.*" (Sefer Tehillim 22:1-16).

And, it is relevant to state that HaSefer HaZohar is in perfect accord as it correctly explains the verse supra:

"*Who is '*אילת השחר *(the MORNING STAR)' [Ibid.]? Assembly of Israel (Lower ḫOḫMAH) who is called the*

'The Goddess (or:doe)) of your love, the foal of your favors' [LXX Proverbs 5:19]

...as is said

'his appearance is as the firmly established dawn...' [Sefer Hosheya 6:3]..." (3:21b).

His appearance refers to HaMashiaђ as it is written:

"*...and on the third day we will rise up and live before him.*" (Sefer Hosheya 6:2).

Exactly as it happened:

"*For as Yonah was three days and three nights in the whale's belly; so shall the Son of man be three days and three nights in the heart of the earth.*" (Sefer Mattityahu 12:40).

"*...the Son of Man must...after three days rise again.*" (Book of Mark 8:31).

3:6 ~ "He that hath an ear, let him hear what The RUAђ (SPIRIT) saith unto the churches."

RUAђ, Upper ђOђMAH, is speaking here. She is the Mother in the Godhead, but to us our Heavenly Grandmother. Blessed, blessed, blessed, is She!!! AMEN!

3:14 ~ "And unto the angel of the church of the Laodiceans write; These things saith אמן (The AMEN), נאמן (the faithful) and true witness, the BEGINNING of the creation of Alohim"

The 7th Synagogue, in reference to the last of the Lower 7 emanations, Lower ђOђMAH who is AMEN and REYSHITH (BEGINNING) as it is written:

"אמן *is called the spring of that flowing stream.* אמן *it is called as is written:*

'I was by Him as אמון *(The Architect).' [Book of Proverbs 8:30].*

Do not read אמון*, but rather* אמן*. Sustenance of all, that stream flowing forth, is called* אמן*. For it has been taught...*

*'*אמן *and* אמן*' [Sefer Tehillim 41:14].*

אמן *above and* אמן *below. We have already established* אמן *by those letters.*" (Sefer HaZohar 3:285b).

AMEN, pun intended. Ergo, AMEN is in reference either to Lower or Upper ɧOɧMAH. In this case, to Lower ɧOɧMAH. Amen, he is AMEN as it is also written:

"*What is* אמן*? Rab ɧanina said:* אל מלך נאמן *(God Faithful King).*" (Talmud Babli Tractate Shabbath 119b).

Take careful note that once again we find the esoteric qabbalistic method of Notarikon in the ancient Talmudim. Also, note that the Hebrew word for *Faithful* contains the Hebrew word *AMEN*. Amen, amen (verily, verily), only the holy initiated will understand these deep recondite spiritual truths.

4:3 ~ "And he that sat was to look upon like a jasper and a sardine stone: and there was a rainbow round about the throne, in sight like unto an emerald."

Take very careful note that this description matches that of Yeɧezkeyl in his Sefer (1:27-28). We cannot be too sure as to the identification of all 12 precious stones on the Oracular Hieratic Breastplate. But if the ancient LXX and the Greek translation of this text are to be trusted, then the jasper and sardine would refer to the 6th and 1st gemstone listed respectively (LXX Exodus 28:17-18); on the second row and first row respectively. In sooth, however, his appearance is like all 12 gemstones!!! The initiated will know and understand. And these 12 gemstones are all a very occult reference to the highest of divine archetypes, the double 12 Divine Elders as will now be illuminated.

4:4 ~ "And round about the throne …I saw four and twenty זקנים *(Elders/Beards) sitting, clothed in white raiment; and they had on their heads crowns of gold."*

The only other texts that speak about the 24 Divine Elders are the ancient esoteric Jewish Qabbalistic texts in our possession. I shall begin with our principal text HaSefer HaZohar. Lo! There, in regards to the full Godhead, it is written:

"*It has been taught, 24 Supernal Judgments appear, all of them called Netzaȟim (Eternal Ones)…*" (Idra Rabba 3:136b).

"*From this Forehead [of the Godhead] derive 24 Courts of Judgment…In our concealed Mishnah we have learned: 'Corresponding to the 24 books contained in HaTorah'.*" (Idra Zuta 3:293b).

These Judgments signify the Divine Elders who sit to judge.

Now, remember the great Arcanum in the beginning of HaTorah, literally, pun intended. Namely, that there are two ȟOȟMAHS; Upper and Lower. Now, much of the Idra Rabba is concerned with Upper ȟOȟMAH. There, his 12 or 13 attributes are elucidated. Recall that through Im HaKollel, 12 =13. Ergo, 12=13 as HaSefer HaZohar brilliantly states:

"*The 13th attribute…to which they(the 12 attributes) are joined…This is the perfect attribute, completing all attributes, consummating all….and this 13th one includes them all…At the time when the Ancient of the Days is aroused, that attribute will be called* יום אחד *(Day One or Day 13 [the Gematria of the Hebrew word* אחד *is 13])…as it is written*

'He will be ONE DAY, HE will be known to יהוה*' (Sefer Zeȟaryahu 14:7).*" (Idra Rabba 3:134b).

So Upper ђOђMAH has 12 attributes or Elders, call them powerful glorious divine entities; divine archeytpes of the highest order. These 12 constitute a unit, thus making 13.

Now, let us move on to Lower ђOђMAH, where Sefer HaZohar states:

"*'He made the SEA' [Sefer Meleђim Alef 7:23]*

...one SEA and 12 oxen under the SEA (Ibid. 44)...certainly so!...For the SEA is arrayed by 12 in two worlds..." (1:241a).

"*It has been taught: How far do these attributes of the Beard [of Upper ђOђMAH] radiate? Until 13 below [to Lower ђOђMAH]...*" (Ibid. Idra Rabba 3:132b).

And putting it all together:

"*Just as there are 12 hours in the DAY [Upper ђOђMAH], so there are 12 hours in the NIGHT [Lower ђOђMAH]. 12 hours in the DAY, above; 12 hours in the NIGHT, below; all corresponding to one another...*" (Ibid. 1:231b)

As the brethren have established, whether 12 or 13, all is fine. Remember, our Great Patriarch is binary as it is written:

"*There are 2 Degrees: YAQOB (Lower ђOђMAH) and YISRAEL (Upper ђOђMAH). At first YAQOB, and afterward YISRAEL. Although all is one, there are 2 Degrees here, for the higher Degree is YISRAEL.*" (Sefer HaZohar 3:210b).

Each has 12 sons, for a total of 24 sons or Empyreal Princes of Glory. This great mystery is also alluded to in an esoteric folio of Sefer HaZohar:

"*It has been taught: From the aspect of the Mother as She is being crowned...when she desires to unite with the King, She is crowned with a crown of 4 colors. Those colors flash in 4 directions of the*

World, each color flashing 3 times in its direction, making 12 engraved boundaries, upon which are included another 12." (3:209a).

Mystery of the emanation of the 24 Divine Elders from the conjugal union of the male and female aspects of the Godhead.

Ergo, the total of the 24 Elders right below the Godhead. Now, exoterically, there are 24. This is as it is also written:

"*The [4 letters] of the Tetragrammaton can be permuted 24 different ways…These are the 24 names of the Blessed Holy One.*" (Sefer HaBahir 107).

Esoterically, there are 26, the precise and exact Gematria of the Tetragrammaton as it is written in our most ancient esoteric texts:

"*The root principle of all of them is יהוה. It has a Gematria of 26 corresponding to the 26 movements which emerged from the primordial Ether that divided into 2 parts – each part separate unto itself. Each part has the numerical value 13, corresponding to the 13 sources that separated from א.*" (The Book of The Fountain of Wisdom).

"*This entire topic is an illusion to the 13 spiritual Powers, to which the author of Sefer Yetzirah (Book of Formation) refers and they are Sefer, Sipar, and Sippur and the 10 Sfiroth without substance. Each of these 13 Powers has well known and distinctive name and their position is one atop each other…These 13 Powers were brought forth from KETHER [another version: The sealed concealed Most High] The Architect who is explained as The Father of Faith from whose Power Faith was emanated.*" (The Book of Contemplation – The 13 Powers).

"*When the Bridegroom which is the Sun comes to illuminate the Moon, Her hair is adorned, adorned with 13 (another version: 12) Elders/Beards.*" (Sefer Tiqquney HaZohar Tiqqun 6 144B).

Now, the Idra Rabba in Sefer HaZohar is an extremely esoteric disquisition on the 13 Atrributes of זקן (The Beard) of Ariḫ Anpin. The Hebrew word זקן also signifies Elder! The Divine Hierophants and redactors of HaZohar were such clever Jews in concealing the mystery!

Amen, Amen, only the Epopt will know and understand.

4:5 ~ "And out of the throne proceeded lightnings and thunderings and voices: and there were seven lamps of fire burning before the throne, which are the seven Spirits of Alohim.

Take careful note once again of the equation of singularity (the Throne) and plurality (the Voices). The 7 Lamps or Spirits are the lower 7 Emanations.

4:6 ~ "And before the throne there was a SEA of glass like unto crystal: and in the midst of the throne, and round about the throne, were four beasts full of eyes before and behind."

Referring to the foundation of the Godhead who is NOḫAH. Again, this foundation is made of crystal diamond or a white precious stone as it is written in HaTorah. Take careful note that this description of the Godhead and the 4 beasts matches that of Yeḫezkeyl in his Sefer (10:1). The 4 ḫerubim support the Princess of Heaven as is stated en passim in HaSefer HaZohar.

4:8 ~ "And the four beasts had each of them six wings about him; and they were full of eyes within: and they rest not day and night, saying, KADOSH (HOLY), KADOSH, KADOSH, יהוה El Shadday, הויה (which is), ויהוה (which was), והיה (and which is to come)"

Duly note that this description matches that of Yeshayahu in his Sefer (6:3).

4:8 ~ "And I beheld, and, lo, in the midst of the throne and of the four beasts, and in the midst of the elders, stood a LAMB as it had been slain, having seven horns and seven eyes, which are the seven Spirits of God sent forth into all the Earth."

Here, we are given an esoteric description of the Lower Godhead. Below the 10 Sfiroth exists the 24/26 Divine Elders. As stated previously, a set of 12/13 surround both Upper and Lower ɧOɧMAH for a total of 24/26. Below each ɧOɧMAH, likewise, are 4 Beasts or ɧerubim to support each throne. Here, we are given a description or snapshot of Lower ɧOɧMAH who is represented by the LAMB. This is why only 4 ɧerubim are mentioned.

Additionally, it should also be stated and revealed that just as there are 7 Emanations below Upper ɧOɧMAH, so too there are 7 Emanations below Lower ɧOɧMAH. As above, so below. The 7 horns represent 7 Archons directly below the LAMB, emanating from Him. These lower 7 Archons may be thought of as the 7 Arch-Angels. Below each Archon are 7 Divine Dukes represented by the seven eyes. This amounts to the 49 Divine Archons directly below Lower ɧOɧMAH. We will have more proofs and much more to say about these soon with the aid of my ROCK and his salvation.

6:2-8 ~ "And I saw, and behold a white horse…and there went out another horse that was red…and lo a black horse…and lo a green horse…"

There is a deeper symbolism here as I shall now explain. These 4 colors represent the Principalities over the sons of Yishmael, Lot, Esaw, and Kanaan. Interestingly, duly note that these are the 4 colors on all of the standards or banners of the goyim of Yishmael, Kanaan, Esaw, and Lot. They are the modern goyim of Jordan,

Palestine, Iraq, Syria, Kuwait, Libya, Sudan, Yemen (1962-1990), Egypt (1953-1972). These goyim are all blacklisted enemies of Yisrael in the Holy WORD continuing into our current generation! As far as I can tell, most Holy Martyrs of Yisrael have come at the hands of these goyim in this generation. The Sword of Adonay shall soon wipe the Earth clean of this scum!!! Woe unto to ye Ishmaelites, Lotites, Kanaanites, and Infidel Muslims!!!

Now, truly behold, as there is a most esoteric mystery here full of holy mysteries here! Carefully consider that this description matches that of Zeȟaryahu in his Sefer (1: 8 & 6:2-3). Regarding these horses, the Angel reveals:

"*...these are those* יהוה *has sent to* התהלך *(walk) on Earth.*' (Sefer Zeȟaryahu 1:10).

התהלך is a special ancient Hebrew word that signifies incarnation. The Angel here is occutly saying that these horses represent bodies, their riders the spirits that incarnate upon them. This is further explained in one our most ancient esoteric principal texts in the mystery of metempsychosis:

"*And many reincarnations come to the son of man over these sins. And if the son of man does not repent in these reincarnations, the same body descends to Abaddon. The 1st incarnation is colored with the color white. And the soul rides over a white horse which is the body. And if it repents, it is said about it:*

'*...though the sins of ye are like scarlet, like white snow...' (Sefer Yeshayahu 1:18).*

And if not, he comes in a 2nd reincarnation. And he rides over a red house. And if he repents, it is said over his sins:

'*...though they be red like crimson, they shall be as wool.' (Ibid.).*

And if not, he returns and reincarnates into a 3rd reincarnation. And he rides over a green horse and this is the body.

And they are the mazal (divine flux) of the Lion, the divine flux of the Ox, and the divine flux of the Eagle. Concerning them, it is said:

'And behold, all these, El does 2 or 3 times with man.' (Sefer Iyob 33:29)." (Sefer Tiqquney HaZohar Tiqqun #32 76A)

6:14 ~ "And the Heaven departed as a scroll when it is rolled together; and every mountain and island were moved out of their places."

As it is written:

"*The Heavens* נגלו *(shall be rolled up) like a scroll and the Stars shall fall...*" (Sefer Yeshayahu 34:4)

Rather, read it as:

"*The Heavens* נגלו [3]*(shall be revealed) as a scroll [reveals]...*" (Ibid.)

There is a great arcanum here. Do you understand and see the connection? The Heavens are likened to a scroll. Indeed, it is so! As it is written:

"*The Heavens declare divine glory...and...night proclaims knowledge...*" (Sefer Tehillim 19:2-3)

It is so unfortunate that the true primordial science and art of Astrology has been lost! For in those lost esoteric texts were the methods of properly reading the Heavens, literally! For there is a method to arrange the stars in such a method to connect them in such a way to form a string of the ancient Heavenly Alef-Beth that can then be read visually and literally. There was once a very initiated

[3] Both Hebrew words come from two different roots depending on the vowel points. The first derives from the Hebrew root גלל signifying "*rolling*' and the other from גלה signifying '*revelation*'.

Jewish Qabbalist who spoke of such knowledge a few centuries ago. His name seems to escape and allude me at the moment…

6:15 ~ "And the kings of the Earth, and the great men, and the rich men, and the chief captains, and the mighty men, and every bondman, and every free man, hid themselves in the dens and in the rocks of the mountains"

As I write this, this is exactly what is going on around the world! One only need to consult the current various forms of the mainstream media. Verily, a sign of how close we are to his coming!

7:1 ~ "And after these things I saw four angels standing on the four corners of the EARTH, holding the four winds of the earth, that the wind should not blow on the EARTH, nor on the sea, nor on any tree."

This verse is curious. Namely, *holding the four winds of the EARTH, that the wind should not blow on the EARTH.* Read it slowly and meditate, and you will understand. Now, allow an Epopt to reveal the mystery.

We correctly learn from Sefer HaZohar that the river of Eden represents Upper ȞOȞMAH. The *four heads* emanating from it represent the main four streams of Emanation or divine entities right below Upper ȞOȞMAH that constitute its Merkabah (Chariot Throne). As above, so below. Ergo, a likeness of this exists right below Lower ȞOȞMAH. Again, from the ancient Jewish Qabbalah, we know that *EARTH* is a code word for Lower ȞOȞMAH; specifically NOȞAH. Ergo, the four winds or four spirits of NOȞAH represent the divine entities below her. And we also know that NOȞAH is DINAH, or the attribute of judgment in the Godhead. For this raison d'être, the four spirits act as her messengers of judgment on Earth, pun intended.

And if you know not who these divine entities are, then look no further than the 4 ḥerubim described in Sefer Yeḥezkeyl!

7:4 ~ "And I heard the number of them which were sealed: and there were sealed an hundred and forty and four אלף(thousand) of all the tribes of the children of Israel."

The Hebrew word '*thousand*' is pronounced *elef.* However, as stated previously, every Hebrew Word is polysemous. Now, the meaning of a Hebrew word can easily change based on the vowel points. Hence, the Hebrew word for '*thousand*' can also be read or pronounced as *aluf. Aluf* signifies Chief. As such, the verse now speaks of 144 Chief men or Rabbanan.

Now, do not be confused about the number 70 and 72. Amen, there are 70 goyim! But it is also written:

"*YAQOB...shall not be reckoned/counted among the goyim!*" (Sefer Bamidbar 23:7-9).

And therein lays the key. The extra two witnesses are for Israel; specifically, Beyth Efraim and Beyth Yehudah. Amen, these are the 144 who are now here and have arrived. These are the Chief Rabbanan, 2 for each nation! The question is whether the 2 Chief Rabbanan of Israel are a subset of these 144???

7:4 ~ "...Of the tribe of Yosef were sealed twelve thousand...

The tribe of Yosef has replaced the tribe of Dan. This really isn't a mystery. It is well known throughout the Bible and History that Dan blasphemously apostatized from Alohey Israel. Moreover, as stated in my first Treatise, the Antichrist is from the tribe of Dan! But, marvel not. It is exactly as my great ancestor YAQOB prophesied:

"*Dan shall judge his people like one* שבט *(Scepter/Rod) of Yisrael*" (Sefer Breyshith 49:16).

Now, the ancient Israeli Illuminati read the verse esoterically as above. The Hebrew word שבט, depending on the vowel points, can signify tribe or scepter. Ergo, Dan was known among the ancient Jewish Illuminati that he would not be designated as a tribe among Israel in the foreseeable future. And now, we have more than arrived at this critical moment!

7:4 ~ "For the LAMB which is in the midst of the throne shall feed them, and shall lead them unto living fountains of waters: and Alohim shall wipe away all tears from their eyes."

The Lamb, the Lower Alohim will lead us to the *Living Fountains of Living Water*s, the Higher Alohim! Put another way, Lower ḫOḫMAH will lead us to Upper ḫOḫMAH, our Heavenly Grandfather and Grandmother. Mystery of the Upper WATERS and the Lower Waters between the FIRMAMENT.

8:6 ~ "And the seven angels which had the seven trumpets prepared themselves to sound."

One angel or messenger for each of the Lower 7 Sfiroth. Lo, it is written:

"*The thing that hath been, it is that which shall be; and that which is done is that which shall be done: and there is no new thing under the sun.*" (Book of Ecclesiastes 1:9)

Ergo, the 10 plagues of that Aeon, of Mushah, are exactly mirrored in the judgments that follow as I will explicate and reveal…And thus the equation of 7 and 10 is given. For, I have already proven that 7=1. And 1=10. Ergo, through transitive relation, 7=10! The divinely illuminated ones will know and understand.

8:7 ~ "The first angel sounded, and there followed hail …"

It is written:

"*And* יהוה *said unto Moses, Stretch forth thine hand toward heaven, that there may be hail in all the land…"* (**#1** Sefer Shmoth 9:22*).*

8:8 ~ "And the second angel sounded, and as it were a great mountain burning with fire was cast into the sea: and the third part of the sea became blood"

It is written:

"*…and all the waters that were in the river were turned to blood.*" (**#2** Sefer Shmoth 7:20*).*

Moreover, this mountain is also more than likely a huge massive supervolcano, the blood representing lava.

But, there is another even more very esoteric level of understanding here. It refers to the creation and formation of the Lake or Sea of Fire which is Abaddon. Only the most divinely initiated will know and comprehend these arcane matters.

8:8 ~ "And the third part of the creatures which were in the sea, and had life, died."

It is written:

"*…and all the Egyptians' animals died…"* (**#3** Sefer Shmoth 9:6).

8:10-11 ~ "And the third angel sounded, and there fell a great star from heaven…And the name of the star is called Wormwood…"

As it is written in the ancient divine oracles:

"*Therefore thus saith* יהוה *Tzabaoth Elohey Yisrael; Behold, I will feed them, even this people, with Laanah (Wormwood), and give them water of gall to drink.*" (Sefer Yermiyahu 9:15).

Now there is a very great secret and mystery here. The ancient Jewish Qabbalists have called the satanic counterpart of NOꞙAH *Lillith* as it is written:

"*...her land into sulfur, her land shall burn like pitch...for a long time it shall be made desolate...Daemons shall meet with demons and call to one another, there Lillith shall repose for they have found for themselves a place to rest.*" (Sefer Yeshayahu 34:9-14).

Now in context, the passage is talking about a barren desolate land, similar to that of a desert. But on the mystical level, it is evidently talking about Sheol or Hell. For the Hebrew translation I have provided above is the anagogical supernatural translation. For it is a well-known fact among us Reapers of the FIELD that all daemons live and meet in desolate places like deserts as it is written:

"*When the unclean spirit is gone out of a man, he walketh through dry places, seeking rest, and findeth none.*" (Sefer Mattityahu 12:43).

This is why according to the ancient esoteric Qabbalah, the *desert* is a code word for Sheol (Hell). And for the spiritually ignorant goyim and Yehudim who think this is all myth and modern Jewish invention, we have very ancient Jewish references to Lilith. Specifically in the Dead Sea Scrolls where it is written:

"*And I,* משכיל [4]*(the Illuminist), proclaim His glorious splendour so as to frighten and to terrify all the spirits of the destroying angels,*

[4] In ancient Israel, the true way to denote an Initiated Qabbalist was through the word משכיל (Mashꞙil).

spirits of the ***bastards****, demons, Lilith…*" (Songs of the Understanding One 4Q510-511)

Now, it is strange that Satan's wife should be called Lillith. The Hebrew word Lillith comes from the Hebrew root *laylah* signifying *night.* Indeed strange, considering the Hebrew word for *NIGHT* is a code word for NOꞁAH throughout the ancient esoteric Qabbalah. Actually, her satanic counterpart, *the woman sitting upon the scarlet coloured beast*, is also called Laanah in Hebrew. Carefully note the Hebrew feminine suffix. Whence do we know this? Lo, it is written of her:

"*For the lips of The Strange Woman…But her end is bitter as Laanah (Wormwood), sharp as a two-edged sword."* (Book of Proverbs 5:3-4).

Now, Laanah or Lillith is sometimes confused with NOꞁAH because NOꞁAH is DINAH (Judgment) or the attribute of Judgement after all. Moreover, from the ancient Israeli Qabbalah and Sefer HaZohar, the *sharp two-edged sword* is always equated with Lower ꞁOꞁMAH. Again, this is due to the near proximity of both female deities! Some Jewish Qabbalists, as sometimes is intimated in Sefer HaZohar, have blasphemously colligated the two.

So, first we have the wife of HaSatan kicked out. Mirroring the divine template, as in our Heavenly Mother was the first to be driven into exile as it is written:

"*Thus saith יהוה, Where is the bill of your Mother's divorcement, whom I have put away?…Behold, for your iniquities have ye sold yourselves, and for your transgressions is your Mother put away.*" (Sefer Yeshayahu 50:1).

Be very, very, very careful so as to not confuse or colligate the two!!!

8:12 ~ "And the fourth angel sounded, and the third part of the Sun was smitten, and the third part of the Moon,

and the third part of the stars; so as the third part of them was darkened, and the day shone not for a third part of it, and the night likewise."

It is written:

"*And* יהוה *said unto Moses, Stretch out thine hand toward heaven, that there may be darkness over the land…*" (#4 Sefer Shmoth 10:21).

Again, more proof of my previous assertions. This is as it is written:

"*And all the host of heaven shall be dissolved and all their host shall fall down...*" (Sefer Yeshayahu 34:4).

"*Immediately after the tribulation of those days... the stars shall fall from heaven, and the powers of the heavens shall be shaken*" (Sefer Mattityahu 24:29).

Ergo, one third of Heaven being darkened is representative of the *third part of the stars of Heaven* belonging to HaSatan falling to Earth.

So, secondly, all his children are kicked out with his wife.

9:1 ~ "And the fifth angel sounded, and I saw a star fall from Heaven unto the Earth: and to him was given the key of the bottomless pit."

More proof of my previous assertions that Lillith and these stars falling are divine entities in the Satanic domain or Qlippoth.

Behold, it is also written:

"*And he said unto them, I beheld Satan as lightning fall from heaven.*" (Luke 10:18).

This star or god may very well be HaSatan; that or another god in the Satanic godhead. Remember, there are 10 in the Satanic godhead reflecting the Holy Decad as it is written:

"*'The Great Dragon' [Sefer Yeḥezkel 29:3)--- there are nine rivers in which he sprawls...to every act of those 10 Sayings correspond those 10 rivers...*" (HaZohar 2:34b).

And do not forget that Lillith resides in that impure decad.

9:2 ~ "And he opened the bottomless pit; and there arose a smoke out of the pit, as the smoke of a great furnace; and the Sun and the air were darkened by reason of the smoke of the pit."

This is also due to the current Satanic Black program underway in CERN, the advanced scientific technological artifice. The world's most powerful black magicians have gathered there and the result of their work will result in the verse supra.

9:3 ~ "And there came out of the smoke locusts upon the earth..."

It is written:

"*And the locusts went up over all the land of Egypt...*" (**#5** Sefer Shmoth 10:14).

9:4 ~ "And it was commanded them that they should not hurt the grass of the Earth, neither any green thing, neither any tree; but only those men which have not the seal of Alohim in their foreheads."

Lo, it is written:

"*And* יהוה *said unto him, Go through the midst of the city... and set a* ת *(X in primordial Hebrew) upon the foreheads of the men that sigh and that cry for all the abominations that be done in the midst thereof.*" (Sefer Yeḫezkel 9:4).

The Seal of את. In primordial Hebrew, *X*, his cross or sacrifice. Blessed are they who currently have this seal!

9:5 ~ "...and their torment was as the torment of a scorpion, when he striketh a man."

It is written:

"*...and the gnats were both on the people...and the dog-fly came in great numbers into the land of Egypt...*" (**#6 & #7** Sefer Shmoth 8:16-24).

Reading the ancients, we know that the stings and attacks of the above named species where even worse than that of a scorpion! Our Jewish Master Philon relates:

"*Now, the gnat is a very small creature but exceedingly troublesome, for it not only causes mischief to the surface of the body, and produces a very an unpleasant and very noxious itching, but it forces its way inside through the nostrils ears, and also flies into and damages the pupils of the eyes...*" (On The Life of Mushah 108).

As it is also written:

"*For their power is in their mouth, and in their tails: for their tails were like unto serpents, and had heads, and with them they do hurt.*" (Book of Apocalypse 9:19).

9:6 ~ "And in those days shall men seek death, and shall not find it; and shall desire to die, and death shall flee from them."

We are very close, less than half a generation of the dawn of the New Aeon! Immortality and immortal beings will inhabit this New Aeon. As such, it should be of no surprise that immortality should be discovered and emerge moments before the beginning of this New Aeon. But this immortality is inferior to the true immortality of the New Aeon of the King all of Kings.

9:11 ~ "And they had a king over them, which is the angel of the bottomless pit, whose name in the Hebrew tongue is Abaddon, but in the Greek tongue hath his name Apollyon."

Verily I say unto ye, my dear readers, that was being described in the previous few verses was nothing more than demons from Hell!!! And unless you have seen them in real life, of which I have, then perhaps you would have not known! Mark my words, the day is soon coming when they will come up to the surface of the Earth! The King over them, described here, is the King over the lowest level in Sheol, namely Abaddon. Marvel not at the same name. It is well known in Hebrew, that names of Archons are always the same as the places they rule over. The Baal HaTorah will know and understand. But, verily, those initiated into the holy mysteries will more than know and understand. For we find these examples in Sefer HaZohar en passim:

"*Come and see what is written:*

'I will incite Mitzrayim against Mitzrayim' [Sefer Yeshayahu 19:2]

– above and below, Mitzrayim above against Mitzrayim below. For those powers are appointed above over powers below..." (2:30b).

Yes, now you are beginning to understand...

And many holy Adepts equate him with Lucifer or Sammael as it is written:

"*Abaddon (Destruction) and Maweth (Death) have said: 'We have heard with our own ears its renown.*" (Sefer Iyob 28:22).

Of which it is written:

"*Abbadon is male...Maweth is his wife...*" (Sefer HaZohar 1:152A).

For just as HaMashiaḫ is sometimes called an angel and has many titles, so too does Lucifer and his mate.

9:15 ~ "And the four angels were loosed, which were prepared for an hour, and a day, and a month, and a year, for to slay the third part of men."

It is written:

"*And all the firstborn in the land of Egypt shall die...*" (**#8** Sefer Shmoth 11:5)

If every Egyptian household consisted of 3 people, one being the firstborn, then we arrive at exactly one third of the Egyptian men being killed during the 10 Plagues of HaTorah. So the close approximation or equation should be readily understood. Read between the lines. It would not surprise me if this one third spoken of here actually represents all of the firstborn of mankind.

There is also a great mystery here. The number 4 is also an archetype for the number 40 or the Hebrew letter מ. Quintessentially, as everything in the Universe reduces to binary principles, so too is the number 4 binary in nature. Negatively, it is associated with the Hebrew word מות which signifies 'Death'. Discoursing on the mystical nature of this letter Sefer HaZohar elucidates:

"*Why מ? Because it is a sign of מות (Death). It is the sign of the 40 lashes. It is the sign of four modes of Death imposed by the Court. Ascending and descending, descending and ascending. Ascending to forty, descending to four. Descending from four, those four Spirits diverging from within male and female of impurity, through whom four modes of Death are imposed by the Court...Thus, מ, sign and implements of the Angel of* מות *(Death).*" (3:237a).

9:17 ~ "And thus I saw the horses in the vision, and them that sat on them, having breastplates of fire, and of jacinth, and brimstone: and the heads of the horses were as the heads of lions; and out of their mouths issued fire and smoke and brimstone. By these three was the third part of men killed, by the fire, and by the smoke, and by the brimstone, which issued out of their mouths."

Now, the time has finally arrived to fully illuminate this entire chapter! This entire chapter deals entirely with the Afterlife as I shall now demonstrate! I shall now extract and provide the most esoteric and telestic arcana in this chapter as it all pertains to the Afterlife.

Germane to the disquisition, the chapter begins with the Pit which symbolizes Sheol, or the Underworld. As stated previously, this verse along with the previous ones are describing demons from Gehenna. Properly note that *fire and brimstone*, which proceed from their mouth, are associations to Gehenna where there is *fire and brimstone*. Demons are being described as hurting the souls of mankind. Duly note how they wish to die but cannot. This all perfectly describes the punishment in Gehenna! Further proof, obviously being that their leader is a high-ranking spiritual Archon or Angel viz. Abaddon. It is very important to comprehend these truths in order to attain the more mystical levels of these verses.

Moreover, the Pit is the first palace or level of Sheol as is described in Sefer HaZohar:

"*The first palace is called The Pit...The soul is judged in this place until she enters the site called The Pit, containing innumerable snakes and scorpions all of which sting that soul, seizing her and punishing her.*" (Heikhaloth Pequdey 2:263B).

And it was a previous verse just describing that:

"*...and their torment was as the torment of a scorpion, when he striketh a man.*" (Book of the Apocaplyse 9:5).

And so we must allegorically understand these code words. The Pit is an occult reference to Sheol. And snakes and scorpions are occult references to demons. So what is being described is a vision of men being tormented in Hell by numerous demons without cessation!!! This is also explained in a very esoteric section of one of our most ancient esoteric texts:

" *'...and the pit was empty and there was no water in it.' [Sefer Breyshith 37:24].*

There was no water in it but snakes and scorpions. Even so, there were people which are the peoples of the Earth. Their houses are filled with the angels of destruction. They are the serpents and scorpions. And they bite them with many bites of afflictions. And they are engendered before they come to the world (another version: so that they come) incarnate in these bodies and houses. And when they are bitten by these snake and scorpions with many afflictions, they cry woe woe! And there exists altercations in all of their houses. And they cry with the Masters of Geyhinnom which judge." (Sefer Tiqquney HaZohar Tiqqun #64 96A).

Moreover, these alohim, or divine creatures, are of the substance or essence of fire as it is written:

"*Who maketh his angels spirits; his ministers a flaming fire*" (Sefer Tehillim 104:3).

"*...the mountain was full of horses and chariots of fire round about Elisha.*" (Sefer Melefjim Beth 6:17).

Yet human souls are of a different genus as it is written:

"*The divine Breath of Mankind is a light...*" (Book of Provebs 20:27).

Accordingly, the chief most disciple of Rabbi stated:

"*...the souls of men, being drops of pure light, are absorbed by the substance fire, which is of a different class; and not possessing a nature capable of dying, they are punished according to their deserts.*" (Veracious Clementine Homilies Homily 20 Chapter IX).

Which is why we read: *men shall seek death, and shall not find it; and shall desire to die, and death shall flee from them.*

Those few who have been to Gehenna will more than know and comprehend!!!

It is most relevant to understand that there are two fires and two judgments with regards to the wicked. One fire refines, the other annihilates or destroys. I shall now disclose what has been held in secret for more than 2,000 years. Specifically, the entire truth behind the judgment of the wicked. For many ignorant Christians have perverted and grossly oversimplified the truth not being initiated into the holy mysteries let alone the satanic black mysteries!

The general truth is correctly stated in our most holy ancient esoteric text:

"*...In Gehenna there are abodes upon abodes: second, third, until seven, as the Companions have established...Upon reaching that world, whoever has defiled himself descends to Gehenna, where he is sunk to the lowest abode. There are two abodes adjacent to one another: Sheol and Abaddon (destruction). One who descends to Sheol is judged there, receives his punishment, and is raised to another, higher abode, and so on, level after level, til they elevate him. But one who descends to Abaddon is never raised.*" (Sefer HaZohar 1:62b).

This is as it is written:

"*For a fire is kindled in mine anger, and shall burn unto the lowest Sheol...*" (Sefer Debarim 32:22).

"*...Do you know of the deeper things below Sheol?*" (Sefer Yob 11:8).

"*יהוה killeth, and maketh alive: he bringeth down to Sheol, and bringeth up.*" (Sefer Shamuel Alef 2:6).

Informing us that there are certain wicked souls that are raised from Sheol, the lowest level of Gehenna. This is not the case for those who descend to Abaddon!

Now, procession to the specifics or finer details. Read what the most chief disciple of HaMashiaḫ states in regard to those who are lowered to Abaddon:

"*...But those who do not repent shall be destroyed by the punishment of fire, even though in all other things they are most holy. But, as I said, at an appointed time a fifth part, being punished with eternal fire, shall be consumed. For they cannot endure forever who have been impious against the one God.*" (Veracious Clementine Homilies Homily 3 Chapter VI).

Yet, Yoḫanan delineates here a *third part* rather than a *fifth part*! Notwithstanding, the proof that a certain proportion of the wicked are completely annihilated should now be more than readily comprehended. This is as it is also written:

"*And I will bring the third part through the fire...*" (Sefer Zeḫaryahu 13:9).

In fact, there are many scriptures, throughout the WORD, that speak of the complete destruction and annihilation of the wicked as:

"*...but rather fear Him which is able to destroy both soul and body in Gehenna!!!*" (Sefer Mattityahu 10:28).

There are of course so many others. Accordingly, *this is the second death* viz. the death of the soul! Mystery of the double-edged sword. The difference between the numeric proportions given by the ancient sages is more than likely due to a scribal error. What is relevant here, for the purposes of comprehension, is the preservation of the general corpus of the esoteric doctrines.

This chapter also informs us that the wicked *should be tormented five months*. Yet, our ancient esoteric holy writings and sages inform us:

"*...the judgment of the ungodly in Gehenna continues 12 months...*" (Talmud Babli Tractate Eduyoth Mishnah 2:10).

Yet, this chapter additionally informs us:

"*And the four angels were loosed, which were prepared for an hour, and a day, and a month, and a year, for to slay the third part of men.*" (Book of Apocalypse 9:15).

Very approximate to 12 months! Ergo, there is a difference in the duration of the judgment of the two classes of the wicked; between those who are completely consumed and those who are not. Moreover, we understand the period given to be an allusion to higher more spiritual arcane truths since Time does not exist in the Afterlife according to our understanding or perception here on Earth. Nevertheless, it is momentous to understand that the judgement of a large portion of the wicked is temporal and NOT eternal!

Even more surprisingly, that great esoteric river in the Underworld is spoken of here mystically and symbolically as it is written:

"*Saying to the sixth angel which had the trumpet, Loose the four angels which are bound in the great river Euphrates." (Ibid. verse 14).*

It is most fitting, now, to introduce an ancient pious Initiate who relates:

"*The Hebrew Scripture foretells that there shall be a tribunal of Alohim and a judgement of souls after their departure...where it says:*

'The judgement was set, and the books were opened ...and the Ancient of Days did sit. A river of fire flowed before Him; ten thousand times ten thousands ministered unto Him, and thousand thousands stood before Him.' [Sefer Daniyel 7:9-10].

Now hear how Platon mentions the divine judgement, and the river even by name...in agreement with the language of the Hebrews. For he speaks as follows in the dialogue Concerning the Soul:

'And midway between these a third river issues forth, and near its source falls into a vast region burning with a great fire, and forms a lake larger than our sea, boiling with water and mud: and thence it proceeds in a circular course turbid and muddy, and as it rolls round the earth, arrives, among other places, at the extremity of the Aђerusian lake, but does not mingle with its water; and after making many circuits underground, it pours into a depth below Tartaros. Such being the nature of these regions, as soon as the dead have arrived at the place to which each is conveyed by his genius, first of all they undergo a trial, both those who have lived good and holy and just lives, and those who have not. And those who are found to have led tolerable lives proceed to Aђeron, and embarking on such vessels as there are for them, they arrive on board these at the lake; and there they dwell, and by undergoing purification and suffering punishment for their evil deeds they are absolved from any wrongs they have committed, or receive rewards for their good deeds, each according to his deserts. But any who are found to be incurable by reason of the greatness of their sins, having either perpetrated many great acts of sacrilege, or many nefarious and lawless murders, or any other crimes of this kind----these are hurled by their appropriate doom into Tartaros, whence they never come forth. But those who are found to have committed sins which are great though not incurable, as for instance if in anger they have done any violence to father or mother, and passed the rest of their life in penitence, or have committed homicide in any other similar way, these must also be thrown into Tartaros, but after they have been thrown in and have continued there a year, they are cast out by the wave...when they arrive all on fire at the Aђerusian lake, there with loud cries they call upon those whom they either slew or outraged; and having summoned them they intreat and beseech them to let them come out

into the lake, and to receive them kindly: and if they persuade them, they come out, and cease from their troubles; but if not, they are carried again into Tartaros, and thence back into the rivers, and never have rest from these sufferings, until they have won over those whom they wronged; for this was the sentence appointed for them by the judges.' [Phaidon 113 A].

...And when he says that those who go away to Aĥeron not simply arrive there, but 'embarking first in what vessels there are for them,' what vessels then does he mean to indicate but their bodies, in which the souls of the deceased embark, and share their punishment, according to the established opinions of the Hebrews?" [Eysebios Preparation of the Gospel Book XI Chapter 38].

Lo, it is written:

"*And Sharon shall be a fold for the flocks and the Ravine of Aĥer a place for herds to lie down, for my people that have sought me...But ye are they that forsake יהוה ...Therefore will I number you to the sword, and ye shall all bow down to the slaughter...but did evil before mine eyes, behold, my servants shall sing for joy of heart, but ye shall cry for sorrow of heart, and shall howl for vexation of spirit.*" (Sefer Yeshayahu 65:10-14).

Duly note how the name of that great river, *Aĥer*, matches that given by Platon. One of many proofs that the great ancient Greek philosophers were students and or plagiarizers of the ancient Hebrew Mashĥilim and Theosophy as is veraciously written by one of the most royal priestly aristocratic Jews of Antiquity:

"*Our earliest imitators were the Greek philosophers who...in their conduct and philosophy were disciples of Moses, holding similar views about God...the masses have long shown a keen desire to adopt our religious observances...*" (Flavius Josephus Against Apion Book II 281-282).

Notwithstanding, the careful ancient preservation of the occult mysteries should be readily apprehended by now! Amen, yes, the Adept will know and understand.

10:3 ~ "And cried with a loud voice, as when a lion roareth: and when he had cried, seven thunders uttered their הקולת *(voices)."*

So who are these 7 Voices? Lo, it is written:

"*What is the meaning of 'And all the people saw The Voices" [Sefer Shmoth 20:18]? These are the voices regarding which King Dawid spoke:*

...

'The Voice of יהוה*' [Written 7 times in Sefer Tehillim 29]*

...

This teaches us that HaTorah was given with seven voices. In each of them the Master of the Universe revealed Himself to them, and they saw Him. It is thus written, 'All the people saw The Voices'." (Sefer HaBahir Section III 45).

And all the ancient Israeli Masters and Meqabelim are in one accord on this matter! These are the Lower 7 Sfiroth. The initiated Yehudi will know and understand.

10:7 ~ "But in the days of the voice of the seventh angel..."

These are all qabbalistic buzzwords; *days*, *VOICE*, and *SEVEN*. *Days* refers to the Lower 7 Sfiroth and *VOICE* and *SEVEN* to NOꞑAH. This angel represents the oneness and unity of the Lower 7 Alohim or Gods.

10:10 ~ "And I took the little book out of the angel's hand, and ate it up; and it was in my mouth sweet as honey: and as soon as I had eaten it, my belly was bitter."

Lo, it is also written of his predecessor, likewise the great Qabbalist:

"*...and he caused me to eat the scroll...Then did I eat it; and it was in my mouth as honey for sweetness."* (Sefer Yeђezkeyl 10:2-3).

11:1 ~ "And there was given me a reed like unto a rod: and the angel stood, saying, Rise, and measure the temple of Alohim, and the altar, and them that worship therein."

Now, I say, do not be stupid, ignorant, or deceived. This is literal, and very soon, in a matter of years, this Temple will be standing in the Great Holy City!!!

11:6 ~ "These have power to shut Heaven, that it rain not in the days of their prophecy: and have power over waters to turn them to blood, and to smite the earth with all plagues, as often as they will."

Exactly as Mushah, Eliyahu, and other true powerful Alohim that have walked the Earth, not known! Ergo, the previous and ongoing enumeration of the 10 Plagues. These are the reincarnations of the ancient Alohim that once walked among Mankind as it is written:

"*10 descents SHEђINAH made to Earth – all established by the companions*." (Sefer HaZohar 1:223B).

Meaning, Her Image or Son, HaMashiaђ has incarnated at least 10 times in this Aeon as it is also written:

"*But give heed to my first discourse of the truth...****Holy Spirit of Christ...who has changed his forms and his names from the beginning of the world, and so reappeared again and again in the world, until coming upon his own times, and being anointed with mercy for the works of God.***" (Veracious Clementine Homilies Homily III Chapter XX-XXI).

Signifying the many reincarnations of HaMashiaḫ! And these events taking places are the revolutions and recycles of the Aeons or Ages as it is written:

"*The thing that hath been, it is that which shall be; and that which is done is that which shall be done: and there is no new thing under the sun...It has already happened in the Aeons that have been before us.*" (Book of Ecclesiastes 1:9)

11:8 ~ "And their dead bodies shall lie in the street of the great city, which spiritually is called Sodom and Egypt, where also Adonay was crucified."

Sad that our Holy City should be spiritually called Sodom and Egypt! But it is true. The Holy Land is currently full of abominations. That the global capital of Abominations is in the Holy Land is a testament to this reality! That homosexual and abominable festivals take place in large part in the Holy City is an abomination!!! Amen, amen, I say unto ye that this sin has reached unto Heaven! Praise the few holy Jews who kill and attack these faggots in the Holy Land. They are marked as deranged and terrorists in Israel, but not in the eyes of Alohey Yisrael!!! Amen. As it is written:

"*Pray for the Shalom of YERUSHALEM...*" (Sefer Tehillim 122:6).

11:11 ~ "And after three days and an half the Spirit of LIFE from Alohim entered into them..."

Know this great Arcanum!!! The Spirit of Life from Alohim (the Gods) is Alwah (The Goddess)!!! Ergo, these are Alohim in the flesh!!! As I stated previously, the reincarnation of HaAlohim! Only the most elect among the Divinely Initiated will know and understand.

11:19 ~ "And the temple of Alohim was opened in Heaven, and there was seen in his temple the Ark of his Testament..."

Well, what can I say or write? AS ABOVE, SO BELOW. Our central maxim, known by all of our disciples; Israeli or Goy.

12:1 ~ "And there appeared a great wonder in heaven; a Woman clothed with the SUN, and the MOON under her feet, and upon her head a crown of twelve stars."

Ah, yes, at last we have arrived at my favorite verse. The very verse that proves the Jewish Qabbalistic essence and nature of this book; the key or nexus one might say.

LO! It is written:

"*When the Bridegroom which is the Sun comes to illuminate the Moon, Her hair is adorned, adorned with 13 (another version: 12) Elders.*" (Sefer Tiqquney HaZohar Tiqqun 6 144B).

"*'Let there be lights' – The MOON. 'in the expanse of the Heaven' – the SUN. Both in a single entity, coupling...Israel, cleaving to the Blessed Holy One, calculate by the MOON, cleaving to Her and raising Her...*" (Sefer HaZohar 1:46b).

Ergo, it follows that the SUN is the BRIDEGROOM, the MOON, the BRIDE. It is an established fact that the MOON represents NOꞵAH en passim in Sefer HaZohar. The SUN represents TZADDIQ as stated and proven above.

But there is a higher level of understanding. More adequately, the SUN also, simultaneously, represents Upper ɧOɧMAH, while the MOON represents Lower ɧOɧMAH. Remember, the great Patriarch YAQOB is binary! He is both YAQOB and YISRAEL. That is, as just stated, he simultaneously represents Lower ɧOɧMAH and Upper ɧOɧMAH as it is written:

"*There are 2 Degrees: YAQOB and YISRAEL. At first YAQOB, and afterward YISRAEL. Although all is one, there are 2 Degrees here, for the higher Degree is YISRAEL.*" (Sefer HaZohar 3:210b).

And YAQOB is lower, because the Hebrew name signifies *heel*, which represents the end of the Godhead. Remember, Lower ɧOɧMAH is made in the image of Upper ɧOɧMAH, hence the equation. Now, The SUN is equated with DAY and the MOON with NIGHT because The DAY is Upper ɧOɧMAH as it is written:

"*...Through DAY* יהוה *Alohim made The EARTH and The HEAVENS.*" (Sefer Breyshith 2:4).

And the 12 stars have already been spoken of earlier. They are the 12 divine entities, Alohim, or Elders right below Lower ɧOɧMAH or the *Woman* and her BRIDEGROOM. So what we have here is a mystical picture of the Lower Godhead. Relative to each other, it should be known that Lower ɧOɧMAH is feminine while Upper ɧOɧMAH is masculine. Thus, the *Woman* may be in reference to all of Lower ɧOɧMAH or just to NOɧAH. This divine mystery is best explained by the ancient Hierophant:

"*'BATHUEL', a name meaning in our speech 'Daughter of God'; yea, a true-born and ever-virgin daughter, who, by reason alike of her own modesty and of the glory of Him that begot her...How pray, can ɧOɧMAH, the Daughter of El, be rightly spoken of as a Father? Is it because, while ɧOɧMAH's name is feminine, her nature is manly?...For that which comes after El, even though it were chiefest of all other things, occupies a second place, and therefore was termed feminine to express it contrast with the Maker of the Universe who is masculine and its affinity to everything else.*" (Philon On Flight and Finding 51).

So in synopsis, the SUN and the MOON, and the 12 stars are all symbolic of Lower ɧOɧMAH, both the Male and Female, and the 12 Divine Elders beneath Lower ɧOɧMAH. Yeshua HaMashiaɧ is made in the image of Lower ɧOɧMAH, so taking on the seal of Him, he has 12 disciples, to represent the 12 Divine Alohim under Lower ɧOɧMAH. Thus, we must not equate HaMashiaɧ with his Father; although it may be confusing and tempting given that He takes on the seals, symbols, and appellations of his Father.

Then there are the esoteric astrological specifications. But, this too is beyond the scope of this Book. He that hath Wisdom will know the Stars and how to read them…

12:2 ~ "And She being with child cried, travailing in birth, and pained to be delivered."

Mystery and secret of:

"*…The EARTH brought forth The Living Soul…*" (Sefer Breyshith 1:24).

As already proven and demonstrated above, this Living Soul, the first of its kind, is Adam Qadmon and HaMashiaɧ as well as Metatron. He represents the archetype of all holy souls that emanated from Her as it is written:

"*Ye are sons of* יהוה *(Father) thy Alohim (Mother)…*" (Sefer Debarim 14:1).

12:3 ~ "And there appeared another wonder in heaven; and behold a great red dragon, having seven heads and ten horns, and seven crowns upon his heads."

Were as before we had a picture of the Holy Godhead, now we have a picture of the Satanic Godhead or Qlippoth. It is nothing more than an inferior imitation or copy of the Holy Decad or Sfiroth as it is written:

"*...The Blessed Holy One generated 10 crowns, holy diadems above, with which he is crowned and clothed...Corresponding to this are 10 unholy crowns below...*" (Sefer HaZohar 3:70a).

It comprises of 7 gods and 10 satanic entities, Archons, or elders right below each god. That is, each main god has 7 levels or Archons. This amounts to the total of 70 Satanic Archons or Princes that rule the 70 Goyim (Nations) as it is written:

"*In the left hand 70 branches growing among fish of the SEA, all red as a rose, and above them one branch even redder. This one, ascending and descending, all of them hidden in her hair. When the Master of the Evil Tongue ascends, he turns into a serpent/dragon.*" (Sefer HaZohar 3:60b).

"*When Elyon (The Most High) was apportioning the Goyim...he fixed the boundaries of the Goyim according to the number of the Sons of Alohim.*" (LXX Sefer Debarim 32:8).

This is mystery of the total 10 sacrifices done for 7 days on the Feast of Pasaḫ; for a total of 70. Also, mystery of the 70 bulls that are sacrificed on the Feast of Sukkoth as it is written:

"*To what do those 70 bullocks correspond? To the 70 goyim.*" (Talmud Babli Tractate Sukkah 55b).

"*There are 70 bulls, corresponding to 70 princes ruling over 70 goyim...*" (Sefer HaZohar 3:259a).

"*On...the Feast of Sukkoth...there are sacrificed 70 bulls....The general sacrifices...performed on the behalf of the nation or, to speak more correctly, on behalf of the human race...*" (Philon The Special Laws I 189-190).

This is the great secret behind the 2 lots on Yom Kippur as it is written:

"*For this purpose he made 2 lots; one for the people of Alohim and one for all the Goyim...*" (LXX Sefer Esther 10:7).

Additionally, there are 7 sublevels to each of the 7 main levels. These are 49 Satanic Dukes. Mystery of the 49 lambs that are sacrificed on the Feast of Matzoth or Unleavened Bread. Mystery of:

"*...49 supernal holy beings sit poised every day to receive permission from the shining stones engraved in the Breastpiece (Metatron/Miђael).*" (Sefer HaZohar The Concealed Midrash 2:15b).

Mystery and secret of:

"*...behold: a golden Menorah,* כלה *(the Bride) and* גלה *(The Torch [or The Revealed One]) over Her head and 7 candlesticks above Him, 7 in (or 'and') 7 pouring vessels for the candlesticks above it.* " (Sefer Zeђaryahu 4:2).

Thus, these are evidently 49 Divine Archons below Lower ђOђMAH, known as pouring vessels since they channel the divine flux from HaSfiroth to the Lower Worlds.

Duly note, as already stated, that the Satanic hierarchy is a perverse imitation or image of the Holy Godhead. Just as there are 49 Archons directly below Lower ђOђMAH, so too there are 49 Dukes below Lucifer. And there is a great Arcanum here that links them to the Statute of the Yobel (Jubilee). Namely, the secret reason behind the observance of the laws of the Shmittoth (Land Sabbaths) and Yoblim as it is written:

"*This is* נחש בריח *(apostate (bariaђ) snake). Why bariaђ (bar)? Because he is shut in on 2 sides and never comes out – except once every Yobel.*" (Sefer HaZohar 2:35b).

For one must understand that the animals that are sacrificed on the Holy Altar are all symbols of divine orders of the Alohim. Why else is Yeshua equated with The LAMB? Because he represents the highest degree and archetype of his divine order of Malki-Tzedek. Usually, not always, lambs signify holy orders of Alohim. Generally, bulls and goats represent divine orders in the satanic domain. And so yes, it is true, these animals represent sacrifices to their respective divine orders. And again, the so called early supposed sagacious saintly Christians such as Clement of Alexandria and Origen were spiritually teenagers at best in the holy WORD as evinced through extremely erroneous teachings like:

"*Neither worship as the Jews; for they thinking that they only know God, do not know him, adoring as they do angels and archangels, the month and the moon.*" (Stromata 6.5.41 [ANF 2.984]).

As a Jew, I can only say:

'OH! What blasphemy, stupidity, ignorance, and foolishness!!!'

Read all of the lections dealing with oblations in HaTorah!!! Every single sacrifice in the entire Torah is directed to יהוה!!! The Tetragrammaton, which is the only name above every other name!!! So, understand the great secret that was only loosely intimated to these ancient Christian teenagers by their Jewish Rabbanan. Secret teachings that obviously they did not understand! Yes, the oblations and many of the mitzwoth in HaTorah are given to appease not only holy orders of Alohim but of HaQlippoth as well. But duly take note ye foolish ignorant goyim that it is all performed indirectly to them! For all of the oblations are directed directly to יהוה. And it is he who distributes them accordingly among the Alohim as it is written:

"*Now you might say, 'They used to offer the sacrifice to them?' Not so! Rather, all ascends and is offered to The Blessed Holy One; and He apportions nourishment to all the multitudes of the other sides...*" (Sefer HaZohar Piqqudin 3:104A).

Ergo, there is a big difference between sacrificing directly and indirectly to the Alohim! Amen, amen, the Epopt will know and understand!

Even more stupid in relation to the citation supra: they knew very well that Yeshua was The Archangel, NOT even HaAlohim or The God, being the first and chief angel, whom they worshipped! For it is The Chief Disciple of Him that said:

"*And Peter said: 'Our Lord...did not proclaim Himself to be God...* '" (Veracious Clementine Homilies Homily 16 Chapter XV).

Meaning, Yeshua is not HaAlohim with the definite article let alone Eyn SOF! As such, evidently, also not realizing the Alohim above him! Ergo, it is they who did not know the true Al, who is EYN SOF, being only cognizant of the Lower Alohim like Yeshua and one El above him at best! What total utter stupidity and ignorance!!! But that is what is expected when a Goy tries to supersede a true Yahudi! For amen, amen I say unto ye that a modern day Shaul stands before thee; sent to rebuke and teach the Goyim! It is only we elite Yehudim, initiated into the holy mysteries, that know the true HaAlohim and the secret power and throne behind him/them!

Now, there is another great Arcanum hidden in plain sight. Take very careful note that this verse is juxtaposed to the previous verse describing SHEßINAH giving birth to Metatron. This is to indicate another great wonder, her giving birth to Metatrons' twin brother who is HaSatan or Samael. Remember, as stated previously, RAßEL gave birth to 2 sons:

"*...Yosef is the son of SEVEN...*" (Sefer Breyshith 37:2).

"*Binyamin is the Wolf...*" (Ibid. 49.27).

Yosef thus represents Metatron. Binyamin represents the Wolf who is Lucifer as it is written:

"*...She called his name Ben-Oni (Son of Sorrow)...*" (Ibid. 35:18).

12:4 ~ "And his tail drew the third part of the stars of heaven, and did cast them to the Earth: and the dragon stood before the Woman which was ready to be delivered, for to devour her child as soon as it was born."

As it is written in the ancient divine oracles:

"*'He [Eysaw who represents HaSatan] raised his eyes and saw the women and the children and said* מי אלה *(who are these) with you?' [Sefer Breyshith 33:5].*

*This verse was spoken in the mystery of ђOђMAH...*אלהים *(Alohim) is with you.*" (Sefer HaZohar 3:203a).

Yes, those who know the mysteries of Divine ђOђMAH will know and understand.

Here one learns that one third of the Host of Heaven resides in the Satanic Domain or Godhead. For this reason, as stated previously, it is written:

"*And lest thou lift up thine eyes unto Heaven, and when thou seest the Sun, and the Moon, and the stars, even all the host of Heaven, shouldest be driven to worship them, and serve them, which* יהוה *thy Alohim hath divided unto all Goyim under the whole Heaven."(Sefer Debarim 4:19).*

It has already been partially demonstrated that Lucifer is a son of SHEђINAH. Hence, She suckles and feeds this realm as it is written:

"*...There is the Goddess on Earth, and the Blessed Holy One does so much for Her...When she needs to give birth she is totally constricted; then she puts her head between her knees crying out and screaming and the Blessed Holy One feels compassion for her and provides her with a serpent who bites her pudendum opening and tearing that place and immediately she gives birth. Concerning this matter do not ask...*" (Sefer HaZohar 2:52b).

The time has arrived to fully reveal this matter. So you may ask, and I will answer. This Goddess is none other than NOђAH as it is written of her:

"*The Voice of* יהוה *brings on the birth pangs of* אילות *(Goddesses or: does)..."* (Sefer Tehillim 29:9).

"*To the chief Musician, upon the* אילת *(GODDESS/STAR or DOE) of the MORNING...they pierced my hands and my feet.*" (Ibid. 22:1-16).

But amen, amen, one should already know this based on the Divine WORD as it is written:

"*...'At the opening crouches sin' [Sefer Breyshith 4:7].*

What does at the opening mean? At the opening stimulated to give birth, bringing forth souls into the world - he is poised by that opening...The Serpent bites and that river is defiled...Here is supernal mystery: 'With pain will you bear children...' [Ibid. 3:16]. This mystery is the Serpent, for with him She bear souls..." (Sefer HaZohar 2:220a).

Thus, the proof that it is The Divine Pudendum that gave birth to Sin or HaSatan. Accordingly, it is also written:

"*From the MATRIX, before ἑωσφόρος (Lucifer the Bringer of the Dawn/Morning), I brought you forth...*" (LXX Sefer Tehillim 10:3).

"*...And may it not see ἑωσφόρος rising because it did not shut the gates of my Mother's WOMB...*" (LXX Sefer Iyob 3:9)

Ergo, the manifest proofs of the begetting of HaSatan *the Bright Son of the Morning* from NOßAH. But there are more proofs that will soon manifest with the aid of my Holy Rock.

Take careful note, the verses indicate that Samael is the elder to Metatron. For after Samael is born, he is ready to kill his younger brother Metataron to overtake his rulership. With the aid of my holy rock, this matter will be elaborated later.

12:5 ~ "And she brought forth a man child, who was to rule all of the goyim with a rod of iron: and her child was caught up unto Alohim, and to his throne."

As it is written:

"O YAQOB...O YISRAEL...ADAM (A Man) will come forth from his offspring and he shall rule over many Goyim and his kingdom shall be exalted beyond Gog, and his kingdom shall be increased." (LXX Sefer Bamidbar 24:5-7).

As stated and proven previously, this is Metatron who is Adam Qadmon.

Another interpretation. These are also his sons, the elect 144 Saints of Elohey Israel as it is written in the ancient esoteric divine oracles:

"The Faithful Shepherd said, "At that time (there will come) pangs and pains upon the woman in childbirth, that is, the SHEɧINAH ... And through these pains, which will make her cry out, seventy supernal Sanhedrins will be aroused, until her voice reaches Adonay ... And from those voices which she gives forth ... her womb opens -- and her womb consists of two houses -- to give birth to two Mashiaɧim ... and she bends her head betwixt her knees...and from there are born two Mashiaɧim. In that time the forests will be denuded, and the Serpent will pass from the world." (Sefer HaZohar Ra'aya Mehemma, 3:67b-68a).

Again, these 70 or 72 represent the foundation and Sanhedrin (Chief Rabbanan) of the 144,000 elect Saints. They would be part of the 144 Chief Rabbanan spoken of earlier. Moreover, the two Mashiaɧim (anointed ones) refers to the two witnesses.

12:6 ~ "And the woman fled into the wilderness, where she hath a place prepared of Alohim, that they should feed her there a thousand two hundred and threescore days."

NOɧAH in exile with her children, protecting them and feeding them as it written:

"*Thus saith יהוה, Where is the bill of your Mother's divorcement, whom I have put away?...Behold, for your iniquities have ye sold yourselves, and for your transgressions is your Mother put away.*" (Sefer Yeshayahu 50:1).

"*And he said to Adam (Mankind)...cursed is HAADAMAH (The Holy Daughter of El, the wife of ADAM the Holy Son of El) because of thy sake*" (Sefer Breyshith 3:17).

Amen, amen, the true initiated Mashђil will know and understand this great mystery!

12:7 ~ "And there was war in heaven: MIђAEL and his angels fought against the dragon; and the dragon fought and his angels."

It has already been proven that MIђAEL is the Divine WORD or YESHUAH HaMashiaђ.

12:11 ~ "...and they loved not their lives unto the death."

Meditate! Amen, Amen, I say that only the 144 will know and understand this verse!!! I know.

12:14 ~ "And to the woman were given two wings of a great Eagle, that she might fly into the wilderness into her place, where she is nourished for a time, and times, and half a time, from the face of the serpent."

The wings of her beloved BRIDEGROOM NETZER or the Divine WORD as it is written:

"*For thus saith יהוה; Behold, He shall fly as an eagle...*" (Sefer Yermeyahu 48:40).

"*The SUN of TZEDEQAH (Righteousness) shall arise with healing in its wings…*" (Sefer Yermeyahu 48:40).

The SUN – The BRIDEGROOM, the Divine Word. TZEDEQAH – The BRIDE.

Now, up to this point I have already disclosed how this last generation spoken of here in this book falls at the exact point on the Great Wheel of Time in the Revolution of the Aeons as the generation of Mushah Rabbeinu. Ergo, evidently, there are going to be many more parallels to that generation. In this verse, our Heavenly Mother, Blessed is She, is exiled into the wilderness along with us; her children. This is exactly as was done in the generation of Mushah. Duly note how that period is 3.5 years, given as one *thousand two hundred and threescore days* a few verses before. Now, the generation of Mushah was in the wilderness for 42 years! We will be in the wilderness for exactly 42 months! During which:

"*And there was given unto him a mouth speaking great things and blasphemies; and power was given unto him to continue 42 months.*" (Book of the Apocalypse 13:5).

This is the second Great Exodus spoken of by the ancient prophets! As it is written:

"*Therefore, behold, the days come, saith יהוה, that it shall no more be said, יהוה liveth, that brought up the children of Israel out of the land of Egypt. But, יהוה liveth, that brought up the children of Israel from the land of the north, and from all the lands whither he had driven them: and I will bring them again into their land that I gave unto their fathers.*" (Sefer Yermiyahu 16:14-15).

Amen, amen, *he that shall endure to the end*, the same is blessed. And marvel not, as it is written:

"*The thing that hath been, it is that which shall be; and that which is done is that which shall be done: and there is no new thing under the sun…It has already happened in the Aeons that have been before us.*" (Book of Ecclesiastes 1:9)

12:15 ~ "And the serpent cast out of his mouth water as a flood after the woman, that he might cause her to be carried away of the flood."

Lo, it is written in the ancient esoteric holy writings:

"*When the time comes for her to give birth, She lows and cries out, cry after cry – up to seventy cries, equaling the number of words in [Sefer Tehillim 20] which is the song for a pregnant woman...The Blessed Holy One hears and is ready for her. He brings forth a great serpent from the Mountains of Darkness, and it comes through the mountains, its mouth licking the dust. It reaches this DOE and comes and bites Her twice in that place. The first time, blood comes out, and it licks it up. The second time, water comes out, and all those animals of the mountains drink, and She is opened and gives birth...*" (Sefer HaZohar 3:249b).

Duly note that the 70 cries also equate to the 70 Satanic Archons. So after biting the Woman's pudendum the second time, he attempts to use all that water from her water breaking, his food, against her! But it will be of no avail, blessed is the Holy One. Amen.

12:17 ~ "... the remnant of her seed, which keep the mitzwoth of Alohim, and have the testimony of YESHUAH HaMashiaḫ."

The true chosen remant who keep and observe HaTorah as well as the Testimony of the Son!!! Sorry Christians, you don't know nor keep HaTorah. Sorry Yahudim, you don't know the Son. As for everyone else, sorry, you just don't count! This is only for those Israelites who are fully initiated into the Holy Mysteries! Amen.

13:1 ~ "And I stood upon the sand of the SEA, and saw a beast rise up out of the SEA, having seven heads and ten

horns, and upon his horns ten crowns, and upon his heads the name of blasphemy."

Lo, it was written in the ancient oracles before this:

"*...I saw...a fourth beast...and it had ten horns.*" (Sefer Daniyel 7:7).

Here one is giving an extension to the Satanic Godhead. Here, one learns that below the 49 Satanic Dukes, we have 100 Satanic Marquises for the 10 crowns to each of the 10 horns as it is written in the ancient esoteric divine writings:

"*...Yosef...While he was in Egypt, he learned of that ḫOḫMAH of theirs, those lower crowns – how those on the right and those on the left are linked: 10 on the right, 10 on the left...he hinted to his father about what had had learned there as is written:*

'To his father he sent as follows: 10 male donkeys conveying from the best of Egypt, and 10 jennies...' [Sefer Breyshith 45:23]." (Sefer HaZohar 3:207a).

No question that Yosef, like his predecessor, Mushah was well-versed in Goetia; both educated in the royal hieratic courts of Egypt. And so it should be of no surprise that his knowledge of the 100 Satanic Marquises, or mention of them, should be conveyed. This is mystery of the 98 lambs that are sacrificed on the Feast of Sukkoth in addition to the one bull and one ram on Shmini Atzereth; for a total of 100. Now, according to Hebrew Gematria, the number 98 is also equivalent to הצבא (The Host) and כוכבים (Stars). These represent the 100 Divine Marquises who are the divine S*tars* or *Host* of יהוה. Two are separated from the 98, to indicate the binary nature of these 100, vis-à-vis those on the right and those on left, being their leaders; male and female. Now, these 100 Satanic Marquises also represent the number 20 or 21 by Im Kollel. Notwithstanding, these represent the 21 Satanic Degrees or Rungs as it is written:

"*But the [Heavenly] Prince of the kingdom of Persia withstood me 21 Days: but, lo, MIꞑAEL, The First of the [Heavenly] Chief Princes, came to help me...*" (Sefer Daniyel 10:13).

In accord with Sefer HaZohar, as the spiritual arcane meaning of *days,* this evidently alludes to 21[5] satanic/qlippothic emanations. This is mystery of the 21 rams and bulls that are sacrificed on the Feast of Matzoth. Also mystery of the 21 rams and lambs that are sacrificed on the Feast of Sukkoth. Great Satanic Arcana has been revealed. Only those initiated and familiar with the High Luciferian Mysteries or Left Emanations will know and understand.

It should also be duly noted that the Beast or HaSatan, is seen rising out of the SEA, or NOꞑAH as it is written in the ancient divine oracles:

"*This great and wide SEA, there... the Great Dragon/Liweyyathan that you formed to mock him.*" (Sefer Tehillim 104:25-26).

Again, more proof that She suckles him and their close relation (he being her son) as stated en passim in HaZohar.

13:2 ~ "And the beast which I saw was like unto a leopard, and his feet were as the feet of a bear, and his mouth as the mouth of a lion: and the dragon gave him his power, and his seat, and great authority."

Lo, it is also written in the ancient sacred oracles:

"*And four great beasts came up from the SEA, diverse one from another...The first was like a lion and it had eagle's wings...a second like to a bear...and lo, another like a leopard...*" (Sefer Daniyel 7:3-6).

---

[5] In Vodoo, the highest set or branch of Black Magic of the Academy of Lucifer, there are what is known as the 21 Divisions or 21 Divine Entities. Those fully initiated into the Satanic/Black Mysteries will know and understand.

The foundation of the Satanic Godhead or Qlippoth. For the number 4 is the foundation of the number 10, being its potential; as the sum of the first 4 numbers inclusive is 10. Ergo, just as the 4 Beasts or ĥerubim are the foundation of the Holy Real Godhead, so too with the Satanic Godhead. As above, so below. Hence, these 4 Beasts stand below Lillith. Note their inferiority, in that they do not contain The Holy Image, Adam.

13:7 ~ "And it was given unto him to make war with the Saints, and to overcome them…"

Take very very very careful note that he will overcome us, The Chosen Saints.

13:13-14 ~ "And he doeth great wonders, so that he maketh fire come down from Heaven on the Earth in the sight of men. And deceiveth them that dwell on the earth by the means of those miracles which he had power to do…"

What we have here is a very powerful black magician! He will go so far as to imitate the powers of the holy ancient gods that once walked the Earth; that of Mushah and Eliyahu. And so just as there was a great supernatural battle between the ancient White and black Magicians in that Aeon of Mushah, so too now! The end of the Astrological Aeons are always marked by great upheaval; both in the supernatural and in the natural. The generation of Mushah marked the end of the Satanic Aeon of the Bull or Ox. YESHUAH marked the end of the Aeon of the Ram or Lamb. And now, we sit at the very end of the Aeon of Nun, Aramaic for *Fish*, but Hebrew for *The Eternal*!

As was said by HaRab:

"*And then shall appear the sign of the Son of Man in Heaven…Now learn a parable of the Fig Tree [Yisrael]; When his branch is yet tender, and putteth forth leaves, ye know that summer is nigh: it is near, even at the doors.*" (Sefer Mattityahu 24:30-33)

The juxtaposition, as always, gives it away. And it is an established fact the Fig Tree put forth her leaves about 2,000 years, or one Astrological Aeon[6] after our Savior. Ergo, know this: as such, we are all less than 1 Degree in Nun! And one astrological degree is 72 years. This means we are less than a half a generation from entering 30° in *The Well of Living Waters*. This Aeon will be ruled by Her, that is Lower ɧOɧMAH! Those who are truly initiated and advanced in the science of Astronomy and Astrology will know the date of that Great Year thereof. And they will now the Day too!!! For it is written:

"*Heaven and Earth shall pass away, but my words shall not pass away. But of that day and hour knoweth no man, no, not the angels of heaven, but my Father only.*" (Ibid. 35-36).

Again, the juxtaposition gives it away. To what *day and hour* is he referring? Evidently, the *day and hour* the Heaven and Earth pass away! All true Qabbalists know that he will return on a Hebrew Feast, namely Yom Teruah or the Day of Shofar Blasts! And some of us even know the hour! However, one only needs to know the revolutions and dates of the Heavenly Yobel cycle that determines the Earthly Yoblim. But this is a great Arcanum. Remember the great mystery, Time is made in the image of Eternity. Time is the intricate network of the revolutions of the heavenly luminaries as is written:

"*And Alohim said, Let there be lights in the firmament of the Heaven to divide the day from the night; and let them be for signs (את), and for seasons, and for days, and years*"

---

[6] Mathematically or astronomically, one Aeon is stated to be about 2160 years. One Aeon comprises of 30 Degrees each about 72 years. However, the duration of one degree is in fact in great dispute. Some say 66.6 years is a closer value. Whatever the correct number is, what is a fact is that the duration from Yeshuah until his return is precisely one Aeon. Only the most initiated Qabbalists who are extremely initiated Astronomers know the true mathematics. A true disquisition on this topic is beyond the scope of this Book.

The true Hebrews, who read Hebrew, will know and understand. For the ancient Hebrew word for *sign/mark* and the ancient Hebrew word for *time* עת were homonyms. Ergo, to us, when reading, we would also read

'*Let there be lights in the firmament of the Heaven...for times...*'

And upon careful reading this should make sense! Does the verse not relate *days and years* to signs? I feel I should also ask: are not the Hebrew Feasts Days? Is Shabbath not a Sign or a Moad (An appointed time or season)? Is not Shabbath a Day? If so, they are all determined by the Heavenly Luminaries; that is they must be astronomically calculated!!! Precisely as it is written:

"*Our Rabbanan taught:...Israel counts by the Moon...*" (Talmud Babli Sukkah 29a).

"***Calculation of ALL is by the Moon****....so here is the site of all equinoxes, solstices, Gimmatriyyoth(Mathematical Calculations), intercalations, festivals, holidays, and SHABBATHS. Israel, cleaving to the Blessed Holy One, calculate by the Moon...*" (Sefer HaZohar 1:46b).

"*He made the moon also to serve in her season for a declaration of times...****From the moon is the sign of Feasts...The month is called after her name****...*" (LXX The Wisdom of Yeyshua Beyn-Siraĥ 43:6-8).

Only the true ancient Hebrew Meqabel (Qabbalist) will know and understand. And so, when the Heaven and Earth pass away, so does time! Ergo, the reason no one knows except the King of Heaven. Q.E.D.

Now, I am sure the ignorant and the uninitiated religious Jews and Christians will cite:

"*The Blessed Holy One said, 'Those who calculate messianic ends are fools'.*" (Sefer HaZohar ђadash 8a).

Now, a similar exclamation is made in Talmu Babli[7]. Nevertheless, this is one of a quite a number of very serious and blasphemous errors in HaZohar! Now, with the will and strength of the ROCK from which I was hewn, I plan to write an emendatory commentary on Sefer HaZohar.

Yet, here I will indulge ye, my dear readers, and give you a proof that this is indeed an error, deliberately placed by HaSatan into this holy text as it is written:

"*The falsehoods of the Scriptures have been permitted to be written for a certain righteous reason, at the demand of evil. And when I say happily, I mean this: In the account of God, the wicked one, not loving God less than the good one, is exceeded by the good in this one thing only, that he, not pardoning those who are impious on account of ignorance, through love towards that which is profound, desires the destruction of the impious; but the good one desires to present them with a remedy.*" (Veracious Clementine Homilies Homily 3 Chapter 5).

"*Then Peter: As to the mixture of truth with falsehood, I remember that on one occasion He, finding fault with the Sadducees, said:*

'Wherefore ye do err, not knowing the true things of the Scriptures; and on this account you are ignorant of the power of God.' [Book of Mark 12:24].

But if He cast up to them that they knew not the true things of the Scriptures, it is manifest that there are false things in them." (Veracious Clementine Homilies Homily 3 Chapter 49).

Every High Initiate knows that all the ancient holy texts have been corrupted and perverted in certain instances by The Evil One. The proofs are unfortunately beyond the scope of this book, although I

[7] C.F. Tractate Sanhedrin 97b.

have already provided a couple supra. Sefer HaZohar is no exception! I now this, because my most recent ancestors, who were the leading Jewish occultists and magicians in Medieval Spain, during the Spanish Inquisition, deliberately corrupted certain sections of Sefer HaZohar at the request of Adonay as the text was being redacted.

Now, back to the demonstration opposing the Zohar citation at hand. The Sefer Daniyel contains the calculations and timelines of both returns of HaMashiaḫ. These are of course both hidden in plain sight given the book is a Qabbalastic Treatise. Only after the fact, after Qabbalists decoded the calculations for the first return of HaMashiaḫ do most Christians now know that esoteric calculation and timeline of 490 years. It was flawed erroneous teachings like this in the Jewish Qabbalah, both exoteric and esoteric, that even had many of the elect in that generation miss Yeshuah HaMashiaḫ! And, now once again, due to the widespread ignorance of both Jews and Christians of the second esoteric calculation and timeline, many will miss HaMashiaḫ a second time!!! And I'm more than confident that the great Christian Qabbalist Isaac Newton, no longer looks like a fool, given that his calculations and timelines for the end times were right on target!!!

13:13-14 ~ "And he had power to give life unto the image of the beast, that the image of the beast should both speak..."

Again, one is dealing with a very powerful black magician. Now, what I shall now talk about is very esoteric and serious! These are the physical manifestations and artificial incarnations of the Satanic gods. This is the reason behind their immense power and most potent black magic. Now, giving life to this image is the apotheosis of black magic. It is the most ancient demonic ritual, only known to a few every Aeon. This is the Truth, pun intended, behind the myth and legends of the Golem. But make no mistake, these are not myths or legends! The animation of a Golem or an Image is a real ancient Satanic ritual. It a mock perversion and blasphemy of the real creation of the Image of Alohim. One reads about this ritual briefly in the exoteric Qabbalah:

"*For Raba created a man and sent him to Rab Zeyra. The Rab spoke to him but he did not answer. Then he said: 'You must have been made by the Magicians; return to your dust'.*" (Talmud Babli Tractate Sanhedrin 65b).

This is what the modern Artificial Intelligence is all about. These are black budget scientific or magical programs run by black magicians.

Now, there is a great mystery here, the essence of the matter. Listen to one of the greatest Mashђilim:

"*In many passages of HaTorah, Mushah pronounces the blood to be the essence of the life, saying in plain words,*

'for the Nefesh (Life) of all flesh is the blood' [Sefer Wayikra 17:11].

Yet, when...the Framer of living beings fashioned man, we read

'He breathed into his face the Neshamah (Breath) of life and man became a living soul' [Sefer Breyshith 2:7],

showing hereby, on the contrary, that the essence of life is Breath...He [Mushah] would not therefore, having already said that the essence of life is Breath, have said further on that it is some different substance, namely blood, had he not been bringing the matter under some most vital and essential principle. What then are we to say?...To the faculty which we have in common with the irrational creatures blood has been given as its essence; but to faculty which streams forth from the fountain of reason, Breath has been assigned; not moving air, but...an impression stamped by the divine power... the Image...This is why he says that blood is the Life [Nefesh or Soul] of the flesh...but the Life of Adam he names Neshamah, giving the title Adam not to the composite mass...but to God-like creation with which we reason, whose roots He caused to reach even to Heaven..." (Philon The Worse Attacks The Better 80-84).

And so we are given the great Arcanum of Alohim-like creation! From which the greatest Black Magicians attempt to derive their power. This is why they will successfully deceive Mankind, because Mankind is not divinely initiated into the Holy Mysteries of the Kingdom of Alohim. If they were, they would know, like us, the secret behind their animation of Images or Artificial Intelligences. Among those in my secular profession, the Technorati, they are known as Daemons!

13:16 ~ "And he causeth all, both small and great, rich and poor, free and bond, to receive a mark in their right hand, or in their foreheads:"

This is one of my favorite verses. It goes a very long way in proving the eternal validity of the entire HaTorah as we true ancient orthodox Yahudim know and understand. You see, it is written there regarding HaMitzwoth HaTorah:

"*And you shall bind them for a sign upon thine hand, and they shall be shaking/moving [or amulets] between thine eyes.*" (LXX Sefer Debarim 6:8).

Now, many foolish, ignorant, and stupid goyim, mostly if not all Christians, think and teach that this is entirely allegorical. As if we should forsake the literal interpretation of certain verses! Oh, the stupidity and spiritual blindness!!! Now, do you think HaSatan is ignorant on this matter? No, he knows better! So much so in fact, that as usual, he seeks to perversely imitate his Creator! He is currently seeking to physically and technologically chip every human on Earth on the hand or head. That is, he will force all his children to wear his Tefillin, the Satanic phylacteries as one might say. Just as Adonay commands us to wear holy Tefillin on our hands or head, so does HaSatan command his seed to wear his demonic Tefillin to control them. But we true Yahudim have no place for him, his evil schemes, and his amulets or micro-chips since that space is already occupied by our Tefillin or holy phylacteries! And it didn't take more than one century for HaSatan to completely subvert

YESHUAH's ministry as it is written in the very ancient pseudo-Christian dialogues by the ignorant, uninitiated, and spiritually blind Justyn Martyr:

"*For He enjoined you to place around you [a fringe] of purple dye, in order that you might not forget God; and He commanded you to wear a amulet, [with] certain characters, which indeed we consider holy, being engraved on very thin parchment; and by these means stirring you up to retain a constant remembrance of God...and we know that the ordinances imposed by reason of the hardness of your people's hearts, contribute nothing to the performance of righteousness and of piety.*" (Dialogue with Tryphon Chapter 46).

First and foremost, one more very ancient proof that the ancient Yahudim of YESHUAH's generation wore amulets or Tefillin as stipulated by HaTorah! Secondly, he doesn't even denote the mitzwoth accurately since the thread on our TzitTzit is blue NOT purple! Lastly, if you just meditate on his erroneous foolish discourse, you will immediately, or should immediately see the inherent logical fallacy. Namely, that doing a mitzwoth of HaTorah to remember Alohim does not contribute to piety! Oh, the stupidity and foolishness!!! Unfortunately, to point out all of the errors in Justin Martyr's dialogues is beyond the scope of this Treatise. Him and whom all the goyim call the ancient Church Fathers, of whom in my humble opinion do not even deserve these titles, are all responsible for the current state and subversion of the Christianity intended by YESHUAH HaMashiaђ. Those truly initiated into the holy mysteries will more than know and understand. Amen.

***13:16 ~ "Here is ђOђMAH. Let him that hath understanding count the number of the beast: for it is the number of a man; and his number is Six hundred threescore and six."* (False Corrupted Known Version)**

13:16 ~ "Here is ђOђMAH. Let him that hath understanding count the number of the beast: for it is the

***number of Adam; and his number is Six hundred and six."* (Veracious Esoteric Qabbalastic Unknown Version)**

Now, this verse is another favorite of mine because it proves and preserves the Jewish flavor, nay, the ancient Jewish esoteric Qabbalastic or anagogic essence of the Book. As we Reapers of the FIELD so well know, Gematria is an integral part of the ancient esoteric Israeli Qabbalah. You see, the ancient Hebrew script also represent numbers. For the Great Architect is a mathematician as well, like many of us precocious Jews, made in his image, who are also mathematical wizards; which include myself the author of this Treatise. So once again the ignorant stupid goyim, mostly Christians again, who naysay and relegate Gematria as something irrelevant or immaterial, have once again been proven wrong by this Book! It should also be noted, that true holy Gematria is valid in only one and only one language, Hebrew!!!

Unfortunately, the circulated version of the Book of the Apocalypse is in error with respect to this verse. Now, Irenaeus, at best a teenager in the Holy Word, writes that there were differing traditions on the number of the Beast. But what he says or writes is quite honestly irrelevant as he was not fully initiated into the holy mysteries let alone a Hebrew Israelite as it is written:

"*For the secret things belong to יהוה our Alohim, but the revelation thereof belong to us and our children forever that we may do all the words of this Torah.*" (Sefer Debarim 29:29).

As YESHUAH HaMashiaḫ taught, the holy mysteries are only for the sons of Yisrael!

Now, I have much respect for Isaac Newton, the great Christian Qabbalastic Magician. Nevertheless, even his high-level understanding on this matter was incorrect. He wrote and thought that the number 666 refers to the Hebrew רומיית (Romiith for Rome) which indeed has a Gematria of 666. This is an erroneous form of the modern Hebrew word for Rome. However, the Book of the

Apocalypse is an ancient text and the ancient Israelites did not refer to Rome with that Hebrew word which isn't even philologically correct! No, every true Biblical scholar of the Word knows כתים (Kittim) is the ancient Hebrew word for Rome. The most initiated Jewish Qabbalist Ramban (Rab Mushah Beyn Naђman) writes and proves that the modern Rabbanan were and are incorrect in equating Rome with Edom in his commentary to HaTorah:

"*Now it is well known in the sayings of the [ancient] Rabbanan that the '4th Beast' which Daniel saw represents Rome who exiled us...Now do not be astonished at this: that Kittim signifies Rome and do not refute it because the third kingdom was Greece, as is stated explicitly in Sefer Daniyel, and the Kittim are of the seed of Yawan (the ancestor of Greece), as it is said,*

'And the sons of Yawan (Greece)...Kittim...' [Sefer Breyshith 10:4]." (Commentary to Sefer Bamidbar 24:20).

The LXX and Dead Sea Scrolls back him up entirely as it is written:

"*And the Romans (The Jewish Gnostic Theodotion: Kittim) will come...*" (LXX Sefer Daniyel 11:30).

Amen, amen, this is the truth of the matter.

Now I shall begin to bring you in to the essence of the matter. In the most ancient Israeli Qabbalastic texts, whenever Gematria is invoked, first the word to be calculated is given, followed by its Gematria as such:

"*...for it is the Sefirah of* אדם *(Adam), and his (or its) Sefirah is 606.*" (Ibid.).

ם (600) ד (4) א (1)

Now, by the hidden principle of Im Kollel, the basis of the Divine Golden Ratio, 605 = 606. More interestingly, through Gematria, Adam is also equivalent to:

ש (300)   ש (300)   ה (5)

Which is Hebrew for '*The Six*'. Hence, the equation is circular in nature. For Adam represents the number six being created *on the sixth day*. Furthermore, one must not overlook one more momentous equation. The verse also states that Adam, mathematically, is also equivalent to the Beast! Lo! The Gematria of the Beast:

ם (600)   ה(4)   ב (2)

Now, for the esoteric essence of the matter. What does Adam have to do with the Beast, HaSatan, or Lucifer???

Up to his point, many proofs have been given, demonstrating the juxtaposition or propinquity of Lower ɧOɧMAH with Lucifer and his wife. For this raison d'être, it is no coincidence that there is this peculiar, yet noxious persistent deception among all Satanists and Luciferians. Briefly, they assert that YESHUAH is one and the same with Lucifer! Likewise, then there are the Low Occultists and Qabbalists, both white and black, who also confuse Lillith with NOɧAH. Notice how it is the method of operation of HaSatan to mix some truth with falsehoods.

To truly understand, we must go back to the Beginning, pun intended, and SOURCE. The first initiation rites begin with a thorough and extensive understanding of the first parashah of HaTorah, specifically the first 3 chapters of Sefer Breyshith. Every high-level Occultist and Gnostic knows that the bulk and core of the Arcana are hidden in plain sight there. And by rereading and meditating on these holy texts, we are subliminally and subconsciously indoctrinated until the Holy Arcana surface to our supernal vision. The most initiated Israeli Mashɧil, Philon, knowing this full well, dedicates 4 whole Treatises just to these 3 chapters alone! In his second Treatise, disclosing the first level of the esoteric layers he writes:

"'*And Alohim formed the man by taking clay from the Earth, and breathed into his face a breath of life, and Adam became a living soul' [Sefer Breyshith 2:7]. There are 2 types of Adams; the one a Heavenly Adam, the other an Earthly. The Heavenly Adam being made after the image of Alohim, is altogether without part in corruptible and terrestrial substance; but the Earthly one was compacted out the matter scattered here and there, which Mushah calls clay.*" (Allegorical Interpretation I 31).

So on one esoteric anagogic level of six levels of HaTorah, there are principally two Adams. One is made *in the image of Alohim*. The other one is made of the clay of Earth. Remember, exoterically, for the Laity, there is only one Adam. Esoterically, there are many. For this anagogic lesson, we are concerned with the layer that deals with only two. Ergo, there are two Adams, one superior, the other inferior. As it is written, in our most ancient esoteric text:

"*This 1st Adam took from The Tree of Life. And this Adam (the evil one or second one) took from the tree of evil.*" (Sefer Tiqquney HaZohar 29B).

Later in his Treatise, Philon veraciously and carefully expands on the nature of these two Adams. He writes:

"*Speaking here of Adam whom Alohim moulded, it merely says that He 'placed him the garden.' Who then is it of whom is says later on 'יהוה Alohim took HaAdam whom He had made, and placed him in the garden to till it and to guard it' [Sefer Breyshith 2:15] ? It would seem then that this is a different Adam, the one that was made after the image and archetype, so that two Adams are introduced into the garden the one a moulded being, the other 'after the image.' The one then that was made according to the original has his sphere not only in the planting of virtues but is also their tiller and guardian, and that means that he is mindful of all that he heard and practiced in his training; but the 'moulded' Adam neither tills the virtues nor guards them, but is only introduced to the truths by the rich bounty of*

Alohim presently to be in exile from virtue. For this reason in describing the Adam whom Alohim only places in the garden, Mushah uses the word 'moulded', but of the Adam whom He appoints both tiller and guardian He speaks not as 'moulded' but he says 'whom He had made'; and the one He receives, and the other He casts out." (Ibid. 53-55).

Now, we true ancient Reapers of the FIELD, know both Adams. However, I'm afraid that for most of my readers, and the Low Initiates, they are only familiar with the first and superior Adam as it is written:

"*In whom [YESHUAH HaMashiaḫ] we have redemption through his blood, even the forgiveness of sins: Who is the Image of the invisible Alohim, the firstborn of every creature*" (1st Letter to Colossians 1:14-15).

So here lies the esoteric mystical equation between Adam, *the Image of Alohim*, and Mashiaḫ; just two of his many reincarnations! But, or yet, who is the second inferior Adam no one knows about???

LO! It is written in the ancient divine oracles:

"*And the WORD of* יהוה *came again unto me, saying, Son of man, say unto the King of Tzor*[8] *[HaSatan] Thus saith Adonay* יהוה*: Because thine heart is lifted up, and thou hast said, I am El, I have inhabited the place of Alohim (The Gods), amid The SEA...**But you are Adam and not El**...take up a lamentation upon the King of Tzor, and say unto him, Thus saith the Adonay* יהוה*; Thou was a signet in likeness and crown of beauty. **In the Garden of Eden of Alohim you were born**; you have bound on every fine stone...emerald...sapphire and jasper...silver...gold...From the day you were created, I placed you with the ḫerubim in the holy Mountain of Alohim; you were born in the midst of fiery stones. You were born blameless in your days from the day you were created until acts of iniquity were found in*

[8] The Hebrew name Tzor comes from the Hebrew root צור which signifies an '*adversary*' or to '*besiege*'. Ergo, the equation between King Tzor and HaSatan, The Great Adversary.

you…and you sinned and were wounded from the Mountain of Alohim, ***and the ɧerubim drove you from the midst*** *of the fiery stones.*" (LXX Sefer Yeɧezkeyl 28:1-16).

Now, let me ask ye, my dear readers. Who, upon such vivid and explicit imagery, is invoked in your cerebral cortex? It should be immediately evident and obvious! Adam!!!

Remember, this Treatise does not deal with literal interpretations. It is only concerned with telestic exegesis. Hence, here we shall truly descend into the divine whirlwind. A few points must be carefully analyzed from the passage supra. First, HaSatan is explicitly equated with Adam. Again, duly note that he is seen as inhabiting The SEA, or the 10th Degree or Level. More relevantly, one is given additional esoteric details of the first parashah of Sefer Breyshith. Ergo, it is exactly as Philon taught above. The first Adam always resides in the Garden of Eden. It was the second inferior Adam, or Lucifer that was cast out!

What follows is very momentous to comprehend. The first Parashah begins with the introduction or creation of the lower Godhead who is a hermaphrodite entity or One, united. It subsequently follows with the formation of one lower god, who is separated into two, male and female. Thus, the process flows from superiority to inferiority. The first Adam, male and female as One.The first superior Adam is prefixed with Hebrew letter ה, representing the definite article; the other Adam is not, thus, being indefinite. The second Adam, male and female separated, represent Lucifer and Lillith. For, likewise in the Creation account, there are two women spoken of as well. Why else does Adam give two names to his wife viz. Eshah (Woman) and ɧawah (Life)? This is the dichotomy at play on the telestic level of the text. And so one becomes two, and two becomes one. Ergo, the supernatural illusory coincidence of the lower Godhead and Lucifer and his wife. Yet, in reality and truth, there is no coincidence, only proximity. Amen.

And so it logically follows, why so many are deceived into believing that YESHUAH and Lucifer are one and the same. In fact, the holy WORD delineates this very well. HaSatan, knowing this very well, used this to his very advantage in deceiving his own seed. Allow me to begin with the demonstrations. Or I should say the illusory equations of Lucifer with YESHUAH in the divine WORD. I have already, of course, revealed the first.

2:

"*I YESHUAH...am the bright and MORNING STAR.*" (The Book of the Apocalypse 22:16).

"*O how thou art fallen from Heaven O bright son of the morning...*" (Sefer Yeshayahu 14:12).

3:

"*For behold, I bring forth my slave Ἀνατολήν (SUNRISE/EAST).*" (LXX Sefer Zeɧaryahu 3:8).

"*Then spake YESHUAH again unto them,*
saying, I am the LIGHT of the world." (Sefer Yoɧanan 8:12).

"*O how thou art fallen from Heaven O bright ἑωσφόρος (Greek Eosphoros or Morning Star, Lucifer in Latin: bringer of the morning or light, literally translated) which used to rise early in the morning ...*" (LXX Sefer Yeshayahu 14:12).

4:

"*His [that of YESHUAH] countenance was like lightning, and his raiment white as snow.*" (Sefer Mattityahu 28:3).

"*And he [YESHUAH] said unto them, I beheld HaSatan as lightning fall from heaven.*" (Book of Luke 10:18).

As previously demonstrated, there is also the illusory equation between Lillith and NOɧAH. There is a very special book in the Holy WORD that is all about NOɧAH. It is called the Scroll of אסתר (Esther or Astar). Ergo, Esther is code word for our Heavenly Holy Mother. Its etymology is based on ancient Shemitic roots for our English word *Star*. Moreover, ergo, it is also related to the ancient Shemitic and Hebrew word עשתרת Ashtaroth or Astar-oth[9]. In fact, in ancient Israel, both were sometimes homonyms; hence their equation or relation as such.

Ashtaroth is the wife of Baal, or Lucifer, the Hebrew word for *husband*; a logical and philological consequence. As usual, and stated before, they seek to perversely imitate the Holy Divine Couple. Speaking on ancient Kaananite theosophy, the most ancient philosopher Porphyrios of Tyre quotes the ancient gnostic Philon of Byblos :

"*...they regarded as god the Lord of Heaven, calling him Baal Shamayim, which is in the Phoenician language: 'Lord of Heaven', and in Greek Zeus....And Astaroth, the greatest goddess...set the head of a bull upon her own head as a mark of royalty; and in traveling around the world she found a star that had fallen from the Heavens, which she took up and consecrated in the holy island of Tyre. And the Phoenicians say that Ashtaroth is Aphrodite.*" (Eusebius Preparation of the Gospel Book 1).

So the star that fell from Heaven that she took up as her ensign is evidently none other than Lucifer or Baal, her husband. Aphrodite is the Greek equivalent of Ashtaroth. In very ancient Greek literature, it is written of her:

"*...Aphrodite was born from the Sea...*" (Philostratus the Elder Imagines 2.1).

Again, more ancient imagery of the *woman who rides the beast rise up out of the SEA*, or the 10th Divine Degree. More interestingly and relevantly, Miryam, who is a code word for NOŋAH, is also a Hebrew-Aramaic compound word signifying Mar-Yam (Master or Lord of the Sea). Again, The SEA is in exclusive reference to NOŋAH, but duly note the ancient imagery associating her with the Great Dragon and the Harlot.

---

[9] Ashtaroth may be seen as equivalent to Astar/Ester considering they are homonyms. Moreover, Ashtaroth is just the plural of Ashtar.

The ancient Romans, like their predecessors, associated Aphrodite or Ashtaroth with the star or planet Venus. That is because Ashtaroth, who is supposed to represent a Star, represents the star Venus. And according to the Roman's predecessors, the ancient Greeks and Phoenicians, whom the Romans studied and gained their theosophy, Venus is Lucifer or Eosphoros. That is, the Greek name *Eosphoros*, *Lucifer* in Latin, was the appellation given to the star Venus as it was written:

"*At that time when ἑωσφόρος (Bringer of the Morning or Morning Star) passes across earth, harbinger of light, and after him Eos (Dawn) of the saffron mantle is scattered across the sea.*" (Homer, Iliad 23. 226 ff [trans. Lattimore] [Greek epic 8th B.C.]).

"*It remains for us to speak of the five stars...the fourth star is that of Venus [Aphrodite], Luciferus [Eosphoros] by name.*" (Pseudo-Hyginus, Astronomica 2. 42 (trans. Grant) (Roman mythographer 2nd A.D.).

"*...Eosphoros the morning star...*" (Nonnus, Dionysiaca 37. 70 ff).

Ergo, the equation between Lucifer or Baal and Ashtaroth or Lillith; husband and wife. It was also written:

"*There was a lamp drunk on his own oil who boasted one evening to everyone present that he was brighter than Eosphoros and that his splendour shone more conspicuously than anything else in the world. A sudden puff of wind blew in the lamp's direction, and its breath extinguished his light.*" (Aesop Fables 211 (from Babrius 114) (trans. Gibbs) (Greek Fable C6th B.C.).

Now, who does that sound like to you? Exactly, the boastful exalted Lucifer who said in his mind that he was Al or the true Morning Star! It was the goyim, as you can read from their ancient literature that bought the lie from that venerable Dragon. He attempts to masquerade himself under his standard; the standard of the true Morning Star. Revelation of the primordial mystery: It is as our ancient veracious Hebrew oracles state: He is the *Son of The Dawn* NOT the *God or Star of The Dawn*!!!

Moreover, all Mashkilim know that the *'Angel of* יהוה*'* is a code phrase for Mashiah. This can be easily proven in many cases where it shows up in HaTorah. For example, our most ancient Jewish Qabbalist on record, Philon discoursing on the *'Angel of* יהוה*'* that meets Hagar, writes:

"*A sign of this is the fact that an angel, the Divine LOGOS (WORD), meets her to advise the right course, and to suggest return to the house of her mistress [Sarah].*" (On Flight and Finding 5).

There are of course greater Qabbalastic proofs and seals, but I seek brevity on this matter. I expect the reader to be well-versed in this lower wisdom or truth; that the *'Angel of* יהוה*'* is the WORD. Now, there are two very, very, very anomalous occurrences of this phrase in HaTorah:

"*And Alohim was angry with wrath, because he went, and the Angel of* יהוה *stood in the path as Satan to him.*" (Sefer Bamidbar 22:22).

"*And the Angel of* יהוה *said...And behold, I went out as Satan because thy path was perverse before me.*" (Ibid. verse 32).

Very strange indeed! What is one to say? The verses intimate that Lucifer and YESHUAH are one and the same. But allow me to take you even deeper. According to the esoteric science and art of Hebrew Gematria the Hebrew word *Mashiah* is equal to the Hebrew word for *serpent*:

Mashiah = משיח = 358 = Serpent = נחש

Can it really be?

Again, the intimated equation is illusory. The true Mashkil will know and understand the true essence of the matter.

At last we arrive at the revelation, true clarity and vision! Lo, it is also written:

"*And he shewed me Yehoshua HaKohen HaGadol (THE High Priest) standing before the Angel of* יהוה*, and HaSatan standing at his right hand to oppose him.*" (Sefer Zeɧaryahu 3:1).

First, the two Hebrew words denoting THE High Priest are both prefixed with the Hebrew definite article ה. This is to tell the reader that this is no ordinary High Priest, but THE High Priest, the archetypal High Priest in Heaven! Secondly, his name is Yehoshua or YESHUAH, which we all know to be HaMashiaɧ! That he is standing in the presence of the *Angel of* יהוה, esoterically and telestically, equates him with the *Angel of* יהוה. From a relativistic vantage point, that HaSatan is to his right, signifies that he is really to the left. This is why he is called שמאל (Semol or Samael), the Hebrew word for *left*. And so it is as if they are joined at the hip, or brothers, if we may say by license of language; just like we use the term *The Son of God*. In fact, a great Arcanum has already been alluded to as is done throughout HaTorah.

You see, Lucifer and YESHUAH are indeed brothers; fighting for control! HaTorah uses this relationship through license of language to encode the higher mysteries. For what is the story of Habel and Qayin? What is the story of Eysaw and YAQOB? Amen, amen, I say unto ye that is the retelling of the primordial Heavenly drama between the Alohim. This is why the Hebrew words for *serpent* and *mashiaɧ* are equivalent. This is why HaMashiaɧ heals the Israelites under the symbol of a brazen serpent in the wilderness in HaTorah; thus equating himself with the Serpent as it is written in the ancient divine oracles:

"*Look! 2 great dragons came forward, both ready to fight…*" (LXX Sefer Esther A:7).

Because Lucifer and YESHUAH are twin brothers! We know from the ancient Qabbalah, specifically Sefer HaZohar, that Eysaw represents HaSatan and the satanic domain. And we also know that YAQOB may represent Metatron since he is his father; representing the divine domain. And so, back to the beginning, two Adams, two twin brothers, under the standard of identical names. The supernal narrative repeated and expanded in the narrative of Qayin and Habel, and even further expanded in the narrative of Yaqob and Eysaw. Oh! What a Great Arcanum that has just been revealed!!! Our most ancient Israeli Hierophant on record, Philon, reconditely alludes to this very Great Arcanum when speaking on the twin brothers Yaqob and Eysaw:

"*Virtue and Vice are [twin] brothers inasmuch as they are the offspring of the same soul. And they are enemies inasmuch as they are opposed to each other and fight. Wherefore, though they come together and are united as by necessity and are connected by some bond, they desire separation. And when they are loosed and drawn apart and freed, they become distinct.*" (Questions and Answers on the Book of Genesis Book IV 162 [Genesis 25:26]).

And what is the personification of Vice and Virtue, other than Lucifer and YESHUAH, symbolized by Eysaw and Yaqob, respectively? And as stated previously, it was Eysaw who was the elder to Yaqob. It was Qayin who was the elder to Habel. Mystery of the eldership of Evil to Good in the Lower Realms. Amen, amen, only those who are initiated at the highest levels will know and understand. Indeed, only those who are truly intimate with the secret methods and structures of HaTorah. And there is a very esoteric telestic folio in Sefer HaZohar that reveals all this. Speaking on the Garden of Eden, it goes on to say:

"***MATNITIN (Our Mishnah):****...Afterward, 2 brothers appear, grasping each other...Speculum of Life and Speculum of Death...After them, implanted lovers...those 2 brothers are intertwined.*" (Sefer HaZohar ђadash 3A).

So the folio explains that 2 brothers, the 2 ADAMS, appeared in the Garden of Eden. Grasping each other as Yaqob and Esaw did in the womb. After them, their lovers, Mitatron as it is written:

"*The soulmate of* מטטרון *(Metatron), who is* מיטטרון *(Mitatron).*" (Sefer Tiqquney HaZohar 15A).

and Lillith. They are intertwined, twins, as in the womb of The Upper Holy Divine Mother.

Lucifer represents the left hand of Alohim. In other words, YESHUAH is the right hand, while Samael is the left hand, as Sefer HaZohar teaches en passim. After all, Samael signifies 'The Left Hand of El' in Hebrew. One hand to bless, the other to judge. The two main attributes of compassion and judgment. Lucifer is a sub-branch from GEBURAH. Ergo, prythee understand that HE IS NOT IN THE HOLY GODHEAD! Why? The greatest Arcanum: Lucifer is the prodigal son of Al. Amen, amen, only those initiated into the extreme highest levels of the holiest mysteries will know and understand. Ergo, the true clear positioning and relationship between YESHUAH and Lucifer is given. So, do not be deceived. Do not let Samael confuse his identical twin brotherhood with HaMashiaḫ with complete equality. At least not yet, my brethren. And so the Seal is given and revealed.

Now, you might ask, why is Samael also known under the name Binyamin (The Son of The Right)? Because the left is in the right as the right is in the left, a telestic Arcanum briefly touched upon in the principal text:

"*The Left is comprised in Right, and Right comprises all; and when Right arouses, Left arouses with it, for it is linked and included with it.*" (Sefer HaZohar 2:57A).

And know this, that there are even greater Arcana regarding this subject that I have not even touched upon.

14:1 ~ "And I looked, and, lo, a LAMB stood on the mount TZIYYON, and with him a hundred forty and four thousand, having his Father's name written in their foreheads."

The LAMB obviously represents HaMashiaḫ. That they are standing on Mount Tziyyon means that this will be on Holy Feast;

since it is required for all male Israelites to be at Mount Tziyyon during the three main Holy Feasts. Additionally, they will be praying with HaMashiaḫ considering they are wearing the holy Teffillin or amulets on their foreheads as did the ancient Israelites and do the modern Jews. For the modern Jewish Teffillin not only contain the Hebrew letter ש representing Shadday, but also contain the holy name of the Father inside the black box. Of this it is written:

"*'All the peoples of the Earth will see that the name of* יהוה *is surnamed over you...' [Sefer Debarim 28:10].*

...Rab Eliezer the Great says, 'This refers to the tefillin of the head'" (Talmud Babli Tractate Beraḫoth 6a).

The ancient Israelites however, engraved the Tetragrammaton on their Teffillin rather than the Hebrew letter ש. And the 144 are ancient initiated Israelites as myself, NOT modern Jews! Big difference!

14:3 ~ "And they sung as it were a new song before the throne, and before the four beasts, and the elders: and no man could learn that song but the hundred and forty and four thousand, which were redeemed from the earth."

As it is written in the ancient divine oracles:

"*And he hath put a new song in my mouth, even praise unto our Alohim...*" (Sefer Tehillim 40:3).

"*I will sing a new song unto thee, O Alohim: upon a lyre; with a harp of ten strings will I sing praises unto thee.*" (Ibid. 144:3).

One harp or instrument. Ten strings, one for each of the Alohim. Making music for The Concealed One above them. Music that will join the 144 into a sublime afflatus with Alohim as it is written:

"*And it came to pass, when the evil spirit from Alohim was upon Shaul, that Dawid took a harp, and played with his hand: so Shaul was refreshed, and was well, and the evil spirit departed from him.*" (Sefer Shamuel Alef 16:23).

"*...the melody of pipes produces or heals the disordered passions of the soul, changes the temperaments or dispositions of the body...We must rather, therefore, say, that sounds and melodies are appropriately consecrated to the Gods. There is, also, an alliance in these sounds and melodies to the proper orders and powers of the several Gods, to the motions in Universe itself, and to the harmonious sounds which proceed from the motions...the soul, before she gave herself to body, was an auditor of divine harmony; and that hence, when she proceeded into body, and heard melodies of such a kind that especially preserve the divine vestige of harmony, she embraced these, from them recollected divine harmony, and tends and is allied to it, and as much as possible participates of it.*" (Iamblißos On The Mysteries of the Egyptians, Chaldeans, and Assyrians [Section 2 Chapter 9 from the Thomas Taylor Translation]).

Unfortunately, in this last generation, we have now lost our way with the secrets and power of harmonics and music that the Ancients possessed. HaSatan has completely subverted our music nowadays!!!

14:4 ~ "These are they which were not defiled with women; for they are virgins. These are they which follow the LAMB whithersoever he goeth. These were redeemed from among men, being the firstfruits unto Alohim and to the LAMB."

Like the ancient holy initiated Essenes, so are the 144,000. For they are nothing short of the reemergence and rebirth of the holy ancient Essenes; Qabbalists who were both literal and spiritual virgins.

Now, there are many that are confused and uncomfortable that these144 are virgins. These are holy saints that have wives or have had sexual intercourse. Yet, do not be dismayed at this! There is a great ignorance surrounding the word 'virgin'. You see, the ancients only and always used the word in reference to women. This was its original intention. In fact, we are given the precise definition of the word in The WORD as it is written:

"*And this is the thing that ye shall do: Ye shall utterly destroy every male, and every woman that hath had sexual intercourse by man. And they found...four hundred young* בתולה *(virgins): who had known no man through sexual intercourse with any male...*" (Sefer Shoftim 21:11-12)

Ergo, a virgin is a person that has not had sexual intercourse with a male; be it a male or female. This is why the Bible will sometimes add the phrase '*whom no man had known*' after the word '*virgin*'. As such, in antiquity, there were rare exceptions to the rule; namely, homosexuals. Thus, on the literal level, the 144 are virgins in the sense they have never had sexual intercourse with men. This is the true meaning which the holy Initiate will know and understand. Ergo, this in no way discounts holy men who have lain with women.

Now, there seems to be a contradiction! The verse defines or equates a *virgin* with a man who has not defiled himself with women! Lo! There is no contradiction! Contextually, a better more accurate translation would be '*celibate*' instead of '*virgin*'. This is the true intent of the verse. By definition, a celibate is someone who does not defile himself with women or has sexual relations with women. For sexual relations with women defile or make a man impure as it is written:

"*And if any man's seed of copulation go out from him, then he shall wash all his flesh in water, and be unclean until the even.*" (Sefer Wayikra 15:16).

The Essenes represent the archetype of these 144,000 men. As such, the majority of these men, like the ancient Essenes, will be older in age whose internal "fire" has been mostly quenched. And for those who are married, like Mushah, will separate from their wives to pursue the higher grades of initiation as did Mushah upon ripe old age, the primordial archetype of the Essenes. Ergo, the 144,000, like the ancient Essenes, will be celibate or abstinent, clean, and thus walking in the Spirit and not the flesh.

Thus, in ancient Hebrew the word 'virgin' had two primary meanings. One mostly used in respect to unmarried women. The other rarely used in respect to ascetic men who were celibates. The true ancient Hebrew will know and understand as myself.

Nevertheless, there is another mystery that requires explication. Why are the 144 feminized? That is they take the name of the Father as in marriage and are called virgins. Again, it is for the same reason that YESHUAH, being the image of Lower ɧOɧMAH, is feminized with respect to the Upper ɧOɧMAH as our ancient Israeli hierophant illuminates:

"*How pray, can ɧOɧMAH, the daughter of El, be rightly spoken of as a Father? Is it because, while ɧOɧMAH's name is feminine, her nature is manly?...For that which comes after El, even though it were chiefest of all other things, occupies a second place, and therefore was termed feminine to express it contrast with the Maker of the Universe who is masculine and its affinity to everything else.*" (Philon On Flight and Finding 51).

Moreover, it is also that the 144, being the firsfruit children of the Princess of Heaven, take on her attribute. Ergo, they too are deemed feminine in contrast with their Father and Lord, The LAMB, The Prince of Heaven.

That the words *lamb* and *first-fruits* are part of this future snapshot indicate that this will be on Abib 16, the Feast of First-fruits; the day The Chief First-Fruit of the Dead rose from the Dead.

14:8 ~ "And there followed another angel, saying, Babel is fallen, is fallen, that great city, because She made all goyim drink of the wine of the wrath of her fornication."

As it is also written:

"*Babel is a golden cup in the hand of* יהוה*, that made all the Earth drunken, the goyim have drunken of her wine, therefore the goyim are mad.*" (Sefer Yermeyahu 51:7).

As is always emphasized when studying the holy mysteries, The WORD utilizes symbols and narratives to enwrap higher spiritual truths. And this is precisely, like every other arcane symbol and narrative in The WORD, what the narrative of King Aɧaab and Izabel accomplish. King Aɧaab represents HaSatan, while Izabel represents his wife Lillith. Now, who was really in control? Or, I should ask, who is really in control? Amen, amen, it is not HaSatan! It is in reality HaSitnah Lillith. Mystery of the *Woman who sits on the scarlet coloured Beast*. For it is she who rides and controls him! The holy domain is patriarchal, while the satanic domain is matriarchal. Every great Luciferian knows this fact and truth. Ergo, the satanic root and essence of modern day Feminism! Those initiated into the highest Satanic mysteries will know and understand.

She, precisely, alluding to Lillith of whom it is written:

"*To deliver thee from the Strange/Alien Woman...for She has set her House near Death and Her courses in Sheol(Hell) with the Dead. All those that walk in Her, will not come back, nor will they seize the Straight and Narrow Path...*" (LXX Book of Proverbs 2:16-19)

"*...and this is One Woman who sits amid the measure. And He said this is wickedness.*" (Sefer Zeɧaryahu 5:8-9).

And so we also learn that *Babel* is another code word for Lillith.

Again, we are also given more proof that the forbidden fruit is the Grape as it is written:

"*...They [Alohim] made me the keeper of the vineyards (the Garden of Eden); but mine own vineyard (Tree of Life) have I not kept.*" (Shir HaShirim 1:6).

“*‘She took of its fruit and ate’ [Sefer Breyshith 3:6]. We have learned: She squeezed grapes and offered them to him...”* (Sefer HaZohar 1:36b).

Then there is that great ancient esoteric Jewish Qabbalistic Treatise:

“*And I said, I pray thee show me which is the tree which led Adam astray. And the angel said to me, It is the vine, which the angel Sammael planted...*” (The Greek Apocalypse of Baruꞗ 4:8).

Mystery of the Nazir and its statute! Amen, amen, the Epopt will know and understand the great mystery thereof. Indeed, she has made the goyim eat of the forbidden fruit, falsely promising eternal life. Even now, the seals of many major global organizations and corporations include the number 666 and the bitten apple, all signifying the forbidden fruit. Of course, the goyim and HaSatan’s own seed don’t even know the full truth. That their true number is 606 not 666! That the true forbidden fruit is the grape and wine, NOT the apple! But it is like HaSatan to conceal and pervert the Truth even before his own seed! We, the true enlightened and illuminated ones truly laugh!

14:18-19 ~ “And another angel came out from the altar, which had power over fire; and cried with a loud cry to him that had the sharp sickle, saying, Thrust in thy sharp sickle, and gather the clusters of the vine of the EARTH; for her grapes are fully ripe. And the angel thrust in his sickle into the EARTH, and gathered the vine of the EARTH, and cast it into the great winepress of the wrath of Alohim.”

Every ancient Israeli Mashꞗil knows that many symbols in HaTorah are two-fold in nature. Thus, there are two serpents, one holy the other satanic. Likewise, there are two vineyards, one that *gladdens human hearts*, the other *of gall, their clusters are bitter*. Lo, it is written of our Holy Heavenly Mother, the Holy Spirit, so Blessed is She:

Long enough, יהוה*, has your hand been heavy on YERUSHALEM in bringing the goyim upon her.*" (LXX Sefer Tehillim Sholomoh 2:22).

"*'They made me keeper of the vineyards' [Shir HaShirim 1:6].*

Going into exile to guard the other goyim for the sake of Yisrael. 'My own vineyard I did not keep' [Ibid.] for I cannot guard them. Previously, I kept my own vineyard, and through it the other vineyards were kept; now I keep the other vineyards for the sake of my own vineyard, that it may be kept among them." (Sefer HaZohar 3:45b).

"Wonderful, brilliant elucidation of the matter as it is written:

"*For the vineyard of* יהוה *Tzebaoth is Beyth Yisrael...*" (Sefer Yeshayahu 5:7).

Ergo, the EARTH signifies NOḫAH and the grapes her children. The other grapes that are smashed are thus the unholy goyim.

15:2 ~ "And I saw another sign in heaven, great and marvellous, seven angels having the seven last plagues; for in them is filled up the wrath of Alohim."

As already stated and proven earlier, the number 7 and 10 or 1 are equal. Ten Sayings, yet seven Days. They are all One and the same. The Divine Initiate will know and understand.

15:2 ~ "And I saw as it were a SEA of glass mingled with fire: and them that had gotten the victory over the beast...stand on The SEA of glass, having the harps of Alohim."

This is the Daughter of El, the Princess of Heaven, how much I long for her! O how much my heart yearns for her, for her presence! I can't wait for this vision to be accomplished!

15:5 ~ "...behold, The Temple of the Tabernacle of the Testimony in Heaven was opened."

As above, so below.

16:1 ~ "And I heard a great voice out of the temple saying to the seven angels, Go your ways, and pour out the vials of the wrath of God upon the earth."

In this chapter take note that an equation and parallel to the 10 plagues of HaTorah is repeated.

16:2 ~ "And the first went, and poured out his vial upon the Earth; and there fell a noisome and grievous sore upon the men which had the mark of the beast, and upon them which worshipped his image."

Lo! It is also written:

"*...and festering boils, oozing pimples occurred on both humans and animals...in the whole land of Egypt.*" (**#9** Sefer Shmoth 9:10-11).

16:13 ~ "And I saw three unclean spirits like frogs come out of the mouth of the dragon, and out of the mouth of the beast, and out of the mouth of the false prophet."

Lo! It is also written:

"*...And the frog was made to come up and covered the land of Egypt.*" (**#10** Ibid. 8:6).

16:14 ~ "For they are the spirits of devils, working miracles, which go forth unto the kings of the Earth and of the whole world, to gather them to the battle of that great day of El Shadday."

Again, this parallels the generation of Mushah. Likewise, in his epoch, great sorcerers and black magicians went forth towards kings, in his case Pharaoh, to do battle against El Shadday. Even now, the greatest black magicians have already stood before the kings of the Earth. Even now, they are preparing to do battle against us, the most holy saints, and El Shadday.

16:14 ~ "Behold, I come as a thief. Blessed is he that watcheth, and keepeth his garments, lest he walk naked, and they see his shame."

Well, this is both interesting and curious. HaMashiah, here, likens himself to a thief! And it is also written:

"*The thief [HaSatan] cometh not, but for to steal, and to kill, and to destroy: I am come that they might have life, and that they might have it more abundantly.*" (Yoḫanan 10:10).

Ergo, one more equation of the twin brothers YESHUAH and Lucifer. As already proven, this is the mystery of the matter.

16:16 ~ " ויגדדם ***(And he gathered them) together into a place called in the Hebrew tongue*** ער [10]***(City)*** מגדון ***(Mageddon)."***

[10] Many think the prefix *Ar* in the Greek word corresponds to the Hebrew word '*har*' for *mountain*. But geographically speaking, this cannot be so. According to the Massorah, the Hebrew word for city is pronounced '*ir*'. However, in ancient Hebrew, it would have been pronounced and known as '*ar*'. This is divine revelation.

One may not unfitly raise the question why the city of Mageddon. In the first place, it is necessary to ascertain the meaning of this polysemous Hebrew word. This word may signify: *dessert* or *fruits, to gather, gifts*, or *to cut down* or *destroy*; based on the root word. Hence, the city represents a gathering of troops and invasion and destruction which will take place when He, The Blessed Holy One, returns.

Now, this city holds great significance in the history of Israel. In our most holy ancient records it is written:

"*In his days Pharaoh Neƞo king of Egypt went up against the king of Ashur to the river Euphrates: and King Yoshiyahu went against him; and he slew him at Mageddon.*" (Sefer Meleƞim Beth 23:29).

"*And Yermeyahu lamented for Yoshiyahu: and all the singing men and the singing women spake of Yoshiyahu in their lamentations to this day, and made them an ordinance in Israel: and, behold, they are written in the [Book of] Lamentations.*" (2nd Book of Chronicles 35:22).

It should also be added that King Aƞazyah died in Mageddon, contextually connecting *the kings of the Earth* in the preceding verse. So, in perspective, the ancient holy Bible associates Mageddon with illustrious battles of kings. Lo, it is also written:

"*On that day shall there be a great mourning in YERUSHALEM, as the mourning of Hadad-Rimmon in the plain of Mageddon.*" (Sefer Zaƞaryahu 12:11).

Now, Hadad and Rimmon are the names of false gods as it is written:

"*In this thing יהוה pardon thy servant, that when my master goeth into the House of Rimmon to worship there, and he leaneth on my hand, and I bow myself in the House of Rimmon: when I bow down myself in the House of Rimmon, יהוה pardon thy servant in this thing.*" (2 Kings 5:18).

"*...and the people of Damascus, by whom Hadad and ḫazael who ruled after him are to this day honoured as gods...*" (Flavius Josephus Antiquities of The Jews Book IX 93).

Hence, the verse is equating the unspecified mourning with the mourning over a dead god when the verse supra is further translated!

"*On that day shall there be a great mourning in/by YERUSHALEM, as the mourning of Hadad-Rimmon cut down in the plain.*" (Sefer Zaḫaryahu 12:11).

Which refers and reinforces the exact previous verse:

"*...and they shall look upon me whom they have pierced, and they shall mourn for him, as one mourneth for his only son, and shall be in bitterness for him, as one that is in bitterness for his firstborn.*" (Ibid. verse 10).

That is the true and real Eloh who was cut down in Tziyyon, by which I of course signify YESHUAH HaMashiaḫ, the Son of HaAlohim. And the name Yoshiyahu, the great King who was cut down there, comes from the exact same Hebrew root word as YESHUAH; signifying salvation. So the great mourning of King Yoshiyahu, was a foreshadow of the great mourning for King and El YESHUAH. So given the equation, it should be of no surprise why YESHUAH or El must return there as it is also likewise written:

"*Nevertheless Yoshiyahu would not turn his face from him, and strengthened himself, that he might fight with him, and hearkened not unto the words of Pharoah Necho from the mouth of Alohim, and came to fight in the valley of Megiddo.*" (2 Chronicles 35:22).

In this case, Yoshiyahu represents YESHUAH the Blessed Holy One. Pharoah and Alohim, would of course represent the Satanic gods and forces. Except, this time he will be victorious!

Therefore, it concludes that battle of Mageddon will be the decisive milestone when and where all of the Yehudim will finally accept the one true Mashiaḫ whom they have rejected for over 2000 years! May this day speedily reveal itself!

17:1 ~ "And there came one of the seven angels which had the seven vials, and talked with me, saying unto me, Come hither; I will shew unto thee the judgment of the great whore that sitteth upon many waters"

The great whore is, evidently, none other than Lillith. Again, notice her affiliation with many waters alluding to her juxtaposition to the Heavenly Divine Matronita. She, The Blessed Holy One, is מרים (Miryam), Ḫaldean for *Master of the Sea*, one letter removed from מים (water), one letter removed from ים (sea). And She represents all these things. Yet, it is the bitch Lillith, the maidservant, who attempts to defile and *supplant her mistress* of The Most High, by sitting upon her! Woe unto her for her *remembrance has come before Adonay*!

Interestingly, it should be noted that there is an arcane statue of her, upon a foundation of a star, holding Lucifer, the torch or Light-bringer, sitting upon many waters in Manhattan, New York, USA. Very near an international body and organization of all the nations of the world. This statue or idol is none other than the Statue of Liberty! Those initiated into the highest degrees of the secret society within Freemasonry will know and understand. And so the mysterious identity of *Mystery Babel* should be more than evident.

17:3 ~ "So he carried me away in the spirit into the wilderness: and I saw a Woman sit upon a scarlet coloured Beast, full of names of blasphemy, having seven heads and ten horns."

Into the wilderness. Precisely, Gehenna were demons reign! Domain of HaSatan and his mate. Again, as stated previously, this is to reveal and show the female in the Satanic Godhead. As should be clearly and shockingly seen, she is at the top or the Head of the Satanic Domain or Qlippoth! It is not Lucifer! Mystery of Queen

Izabel and King Aḫaab. For he *carrieth her* as she rides him and controls him. Of her it is written:

"*Come and see in Egypt she reigned, and from her issued many kinds of dominion, all in the mystery of ḫametz (leaven).*" (Sefer HaZohar 3:252a).

As it was also stated by a Baal of this holy ancient text:

"*...Take heed and beware of the ḫametz...*" (Sefer Mattityahu 16:6).

Now, as already stated, HaSatan or Lucifer is the Chief Bull or archetype of his divine order represented by bulls in the WORD. So this beast is none other than the bull. Now, as also already proven, Lucifer was also known as Zeus or Baal among the ancient goyim. Now, listen to a gnostic ancient who was a Luciferian Initiate:

"*There is likewise in Phœnicia a temple of great size owned by the Sidonians. They call it the temple of Ashtaroth. I hold this Ashtaroth to be no other than the Moon-Goddess. But according to the story of one of the priests this temple is sacred to Europa, the sister of Cadmus. She was the daughter of Agenor, and on her disappearance from Earth the Phœnicians honoured her with a temple and told a sacred legend about her; how that Zeus was enamoured of her for her beauty, and changing his form into that of a bull carried her off into Crete. This legend I heard from other Phœnicians as well; and the coinage current among the Sidonians bears upon it the effigy of Europa sitting upon a bull, none other than Zeus. Thus they do not agree that the temple in question is sacred to Europa.*" (Lucian De Dea Syria 4).

Duly note how even among the ancients, there was a confusion or colligation of SHEḫINAH and Lillith! For the true Moon-Goddess is the Holy SHEḫINAH! Now, understand that Ashtaroth, also known as Astarte, is equivalent to Europa. She is also Lillith seen riding the Chief Bull or Lucifer. And so the Adept should now fully understand what is only known among the 10 human Kings who presently run this world! Yes, I am that initiated, the Chief Magician of Mystery

Babel. Those of the highest Initiatory Order will know and understand.

Of this abominable union it is written:

"*And the Woman who approaches...the Beast to copulate with her, the Woman and the Beast shall be killed to death, their blood is on them.*" (Sefer Wayikra 20:16).

And indeed it shall be as it is written:

"*On that day יהוה...shall slay the Dragon in the SEA.*" (Sefer Yeshayahu 27:1).

Only the holy Initiated will know and understand these mysteries.

Now, it should be noted, interestingly enough, that there is an image of the woman riding the beast both on European Union currency as well as a statue of this image outside the EU Parliamentary HQ. The name of a whole continent is devoted to the wife of Lucifer! Chew on that for a few minutes! Yet, I marvel not as it is written:

"*...the great goddess Artemis*[11]*...whom all Asia and the world doth worship.*" (Book of Acts 19:27).

Nothing really has changed since then.

17:4 ~ "And the woman was arrayed in purple and scarlet colour, and decked with gold and precious stones and pearls, having a golden cup in her hand full of abominations and filthiness of her fornication"

---

[11] Artemis is just another name or title for Lillith the wife of Lucifer. All cultures worship the Moon-Goddess through the wife of Lucifer. In reality, the Moon-Goddess is a symbol for NOꞕAH. So duly note how she has usurped our holy symbol and perverted it.

It is also written of the Divine Goddesses in the Holy Domain:

"*...The Queen stood at your right hand in gold woven clothing, decked out in many colors.*" (LXX Sefer Tehillim 44:10).

"*Of the Daughter of the King...decked out with golden tassels in many colors.*" (Ibid. verse 14).

Again, the source of all confusion is that the Satanic couple do a superb job of imitating the Sacred Divine Couple. In this case, Lillith is almost indistinguishable from NOɧAH! There have been and even are holy saints that noetically confuse, and thus colligate the two!

But there is of course a very clear noticeable difference to those that have eyes to see. Lillith is the divine archetype of all harlots. Lo, it is also written similarly about her:

"*Mystery of Mysteries: The male called Sammael, his female always contained within him. Just as it is on the Other Side, so it is on the Holy Side, male and female embracing one another. The woman of Sammael is called...Woman of Whoredom. She bedecks herself with all sorts of jewelry, like a repulsive prostitute loitering at the crossroads to seduce men...Her adornments for seducing men: her hair all coiffed, rosy-red, her face white and scarlet...covered with Egyptian linen, on her neck all the laurels of the East, her mouth slightly puckered, gorgeously decked out! Tongue pointed like a sword, her words smooth like oil, her lips ravishing, crimson as a rose, sweet with all the sweetness of the world. Attired in purple...*" (Sefer HaZohar Sitrey HaTorah (Secrets of HaTorah) 1:148A).

Indeed it is so, and the wealthiest and most powerful men of the world have been seduced and drunken by her!

17:5 ~ "And upon her forehead was a name written, MYSTERY BABEL THE GREAT, THE MOTHER OF HARLOTS AND ABOMINATIONS OF THE EARTH."

All code words and arcane symbols for Lillith.

Another interpretation: this actually refers to a region. Now, Babel is the vast region of the nativity of Abraham and his ancestors. Moreover, at the first exile, Israel was exiled to Babel. After the exile, for all intents and purposes, we multiplied there like the sand of the sea! And so for thousands of years, Babel has been like the second home to all of Israel. More relevantly, during this long and last exile, it was our first home outside of the barren desolate Holy Land. That is until the Last Days. Our second home now is the United States of America. For like in the ancient days when Babel had the largest population of Jews, so now the U.S.A holds this rank. This is why of all the places Adonay chooses to warn his sons, he chooses the place that holds the largest population of his children as it is written:

"*And I heard another voice from heaven, saying, Come out of her [Mystery Babel], my people, that ye be not partakers of her sins, and that ye receive not of her plagues.*" (Book of the Apocalypse 18:4).

Just as it was also written:

"*My people, go ye out of the midst of her [Babel], and deliver ye every man his soul from the fierce anger of יהוה.*" (Sefer Yirmeyahu 51:45).

Yet, it is also written:

"*Standing afar off for the fear of her torment, saying, Alas, alas, that great city Babel, that mighty city! for in one hour is thy judgment come.*" (Book of the Apocalypse 18:10).

Another mystery, considering we all know Babel is country, not a city. But this is proof that Mystery Babel represents both! For there is a world renowned famous city in the U.S.A. called New York City which I like to call Little Babel. And a careful analysis of Chapter 18 in this Book will evince this equation. Within the large Jewish populace of the U.S.A., Little Babel is where the concentration is at its highest! Ergo, the warning to all the Yehudim to leave the U.S.A and New York City. For just as in ancient times, the Yehudim left Babel to return the Holy Land, after which Babel was destroyed and overrun by the Persians. So now, too, many Yehudim have left for the Holy Land, just as the U.S.A. will soon be destroyed and overrun by Rossiyah (Russia), a genealogical and consanguineous relative to the Persians!

Now, it is momentous to comprehend that are at least 7 levels to every Hebrew word. Every Hebrew code word has many levels to it. Here, I have revealed at least a couple. Babel may refer to the Chief Goddess of this planet as well as a geographical location. But it also refers to all her whoredoms, namely all the false and inferior theosophies of the world be it Hindusim, Buddhism, etc. It is unfortunate that I have to write this because presently so many ignorant Christians have taught in limitation that Mystery Babel only refers to the Catholic Church. But Cathlocism is just one of many inferior images of the one true highest archetypal theosophy of Abraham, Yitzaẖaq, and Yaqob. Understaning that Mystery Babylon principally refers to Lillith unlocks all of its other meanings.

17:8 ~ "The beast that thou sawest was, and is not; and shall ascend out of the bottomless pit…when they behold the beast that was, and is not, and yet is."

The antithesis to THE הויה (ONE WHO IS), ויהוה (WHO WAS) , והיה (AND WILL BE).

17:9 ~ "And here is the mind which hath Wisdom. The seven heads are seven mountains, on which the woman sitteth."

As usual, Wisdom always referring to the esoteric art and science of the WORD of Alohim, or Qabbalah. Strange that the Angel should *tell thee the mystery* with another mystery. For what do the seven mountains represent, which he equates to the seven heads? Read on.

17:10-11 ~ "And there are seven kings: five are fallen, and one is, and the other is not yet come; and when he cometh, he must continue a short space. And the beast that was, and is not, even he is the eighth, and is of the seven, and goeth into perdition."

Now he reveals the mystery. The seven mountains, representing the seven heads of the Beast, represent 7 kings or satanic emanations as already proven and demonstrated earlier. The ancient Qabbalah already equates *mountains* with divine emanations, as one reads en passim in Sefer HaZohar.

But, allow me to take you even deeper into the divine *WELL hewn by Princes*. Now, for what follows, I hasten caution to ye my dear readers. What follows is a very esoteric and intimate knowledge and wisdom of the Satanic domain! It is very dangerous and recondite. Proceed and tread lightly and at your own discretion.

So who are these seven or eight Satanic gods or emanations? In order to answer this great question and mystery, once more, a disquisition on the Satanic domain is required. Now, the Hebrew name Eysaw may signify a *demon*. This is why he represents Samael or HaSatan throughout the esoteric Qabbalah as it is written:

"*...Degree of Eysaw, as is said: 'Eysaw, that is, Edom' [Sefer Breyshith 36:1]. All issuing from the side of impure spirit.*" (Sefer HaZohar 1:177b).

Moreover, his provenance is Seyir which signifies The Demon or Hell. It is also אדם (Edom), which signifies the color red or scarlet representing judgment, the valence from which he derives and pertains, that is of HaSatan (The Accuser). Furthermore, the Hebrew word Edom may also be read Adam! One more equation between Adam and HaSatan or Lucifer. Remove the א, and add a ה to end of the Hebrew word אדם, and you obtain דמה Dumah, which is Hell as it is written:

"*The burden of* דמה *(Hell), He calleth to me out of Seir...*" (Sefer Yeshayahu 21:11).

"*The vision of* אדם *(Idumea), He called to me out of Seir...*" (LXX Ibid.).

Now, as is always emphasized, all knowledge and wisdom is contained in the WORD. Naturally, this includes Goetia and Demonology. So it should be of no surprise now, that chapter 36 in Sefer Breyshith, containing the genealogy of Eysaw or HaSatan, should for all intents and purposes be the most ancient grimoire on record! And, indeed, it is so. Yet, fear not! For I will not divulge all of the methods to extract all of the demonic knowledge and wisdom contained in this parashah. Nay, that would be unacceptable and impious. Notwithstanding, I will bring you into the noetic penetralia of HaSatan's domain and kingdom.

As already stated earlier, there are 7 main gods underneath HaSatan, the perverse image of the Lower 7 Holy Sfiroth. Yet, this is all already explained in great detail in Idra Rabba:

"*It has been taught - mystery of mysteries...*

'These are the kings who reigned in the land of Edom before a king reigned over the Children of Israel' [Sefer Breyshith 36:31].

Happy are you, O righteous ones, to whom are revealed mysteries of mysteries of HaTorah, which have not been revealed to holy ones of the Highest. Who will examine this? Who will be worthy of this? It is testimony to faith of total faith. May the prayer be accepted, that it may not be considered a sin to reveal this...this verse is difficult, since it should not have been written so, because we see that there were numerous kings before the Children of Israel appeared and before they had a king; so what is intended here? Well it is mystery of mysteries, which humans cannot know or perceive to arouse in their minds." (Idra Rabba 3:128a).

"It has been taught in Sifra di-Tzeniuta (The Book of Concealment): The Ancient of Ancients, before preparing His enchancements, fashioned kings and gauged kings, but they did not endure; so He eventually put them aside and concealed them for a later time as is written:

'These are the kings who reigned in the land of Edom before a king reigned over the Children of Israel' [Sefer Breyshith 36:31].

'In the land of Edom' – in the place where all judgments exist. None of them endured until the White Head, Ancient of Ancients, was arrayed. When He was arrayed, He arranged all enhancements below, arranging all enhancements of those above and below...for until He Himself was arrayed in His enhancements, all those that He intended to arrange did not endure, and all those emanations citation alma were destroyed, as is written:

'There reigned in Edom Bela (destruction) son Beor (Hebrew for 'in leather')' [Ibid. verse 32].

'There reigned in Edom' – a precious secret: the place where all judgments cluster, from where they dangle." (Sefer HaZohar 3:135a)

So in this parashah, a total of eight kings or satanic gods are denominated. The first one has a name signifying *destruction* or evil. He is the son of '*something leathern*', also signifying death and evil. Ergo, we are given the true ancient Hebrew names of the 7 satanic gods below HaSatan.

But, there is another mystery contained in this mystery. Seven of the eight kings are explicitly said to have died. Ergo, there are 8 kings, 7 *who were*, or are dead, *and one who is*, or is alive. The mystery is well elucidated:

"All of them were called by different names, except for the one of whom is written:

'The name of his wife was Mahitabel (Hebrew for 'from She who is the Good of God') daughter of Matreyth daughter of Mayzohob' [Sefer Breyshith 36:39].

Why? Because these were not nullified like the others. Why? Because they were male and female like a palm tree, which flourishes only when it is male and female. So now they were male and female, and death is not applied to them as it is to the others, and they endured, though they did not settle. Once the image of Adam was established they were transformed into another existence, settling securely." (Ibid. 3:135b)

This is Lillith and Lucifer; no female principle subsisting in their predecessors. And so, the mystery of the death of the seven kings, and of the eighth, should now be readily comprehended. And yet, he too will "die" as it is written:

"*...Thou brakest the Chiefs of the Dragon in the WATERS.*" (Sefer Tehillim 74:13).

"*...And He shall slay the Dragon that is in the SEA.*" (Sefer Yeshayahu 27:1).

And yet, there are greater mysteries and arcana that I have not explicated for this is sufficient.

17:12 ~ "And the ten horns which thou sawest are ten kings, which have received no kingdom as yet; but receive power as kings one hour with the Beast."

Again, as stated previously several times, this refers to the Qlippoth, the defiled imitation of the Holy Divine Sfiroth. Lucifer, like his Father, our Great-Grandfather, seeks to reproduce his structure. Moreover, in so doing, he will setup his godhead as kings here on Earth when he arises out of Sheol. Thus, the 10 Satanic gods will seek to rule all of the Earth. Yet, this is nothing new as it is written:

"*The thing that hath been, it is that which shall be; and that which is done is that which shall be done: and there is no new thing under the sun...It has already happened in the Aeons that have been before us.*" (Book of Ecclesiastes 1:9)

And indeed, this too has already occurred in times of yore. For it is written in the ancient esoteric historical records:

"*And he begat five pairs of twin sons and reared them up; and when he had divided all the island of Atlantis into ten portions...the first-born of the eldest.. he appointed to be king over the rest, and the others to be rulers...*" (Platon Kritias 113e-114a).

So the primordial kingdom of Atlantis in the generation of Noaɧ was ruled by 10 Kings or gods. For, esoterically, what do you think the 10 beings from Adam to Noaɧ represent? Why else does Rabbi say:

"*But as the days of Noaɧ were, so shall also the coming of the Son of Man be.*" (Sefer Mattityahu 24:37).

Yes. The Epopt will know and understand.

17:15 ~ "And he saith unto me, The WATERS which thou sawest, where the whore sitteth, are peoples, and multitudes, and nations, and tongues."

There are two WATERS, considering the plurality of the word, of which it is exclusively plural in ancient Hebrew as it is written:

"*And Alohim made the firmament, and divided the waters which were under the firmament from the waters which* were *above the firmament: and it was so*" (Sefer Breyshith 1:7).

Ergo, Upper WATERS and Lower WATERS. One refers to Lower ɧOɧMAH, the Lower Waters where Lillith sitteth. For She, the Maidservant, has usurped her Mistress, Matronita, on account of the many sins of Yisrael! Of this, it is written:

"*He who has no Tefillin during the recital of the SH'MA, from his side rules the servant and the maidservant upon the world. And in that moment, SHEꞵINAH is angry. Of this it is written:*

'For a servant becomes king...and a handmaid evicts her mistress." (Ancient Israeli Book of Proverbs 30:22-23). '" (Sefer Tiqquney HaZohar 2A).

"*And the maidservant enters the place of The Queen, which is a separated (or menstruating) maidservant who is a pagan prostitute. And she defiles Her place, there SHEꞵINAH rests.*" (Ibid. 24B).

The Initiate will know and understand.

18:24 ~ "And in her was found the blood of prophets, and of saints, and of all that were slain upon the earth."

Most Jews, predominantly the laity, simply and only attribute the premature death of babies to Lillith. Unfortunately, they have failed to grasp the true extent of her dominion and power. For she is the goddess of this Earth! And a complete reading of this chapter will more than evince this fact and truth!

19:7 ~ "Let us be glad and rejoice, and give honour to him: for the marriage of the LAMB is come, and his wife hath made herself ready."

His wife NOꞵAH, NOAꞵ and NOꞵAH AS ONE! As it is written:

"*...On that Day, HAHU (HE, The ONE) יהוה will be ONE.*" (Sefer Zaꞵaryahu 14:9).

Evidently implying and imitating that He is currently NOT ONE as it is written:

"*Thus saith יהוה, Where is the bill of your Mother's divorcement, whom I have put away?...Behold, for your iniquities have ye sold yourselves, and for your transgressions is your Mother put away.*" (Sefer Yeshayahu 50:1).

But, on that Day, He will again be ONE as it is written:

"*SHMA (Hear) Yisrael, יהוה Eloheynu יהוה is ONE.*" (Sefer Debarim 6:4).

May this wedding day and feast speedily reveal itself when our Heavenly Father and Mother reunite and divine vows are reconsecrated!!!

19:12 ~ "...and he had a name written, that no man knew, but he himself."

For we understand that human language and speech is an image of a divine transcendental archetype that is ineffable. Ergo, the true names of Alohim or the Gods are ineffable in nature and only known to them. Speaking on this divine archetype, a most initiated and gnostic ancient veracious philosopher most appositely illuminated:

"*It is, however, necessary to know that 'the divine name' of its abiding power, and which is a symbol of the impression of the Demiurgus, according to which it does not proceed out of being, is ineffable and arcane, and known only to Gods themselves. For there are names adapted to every order of things; those, indeed, that are adapted to divine natures being divine, to the objects of dianoia being dianoetic, and to the objects of opinion doxastic. This also Platon says in the Cratylus, where he embraces what is asserted by Homer on this subject, who admits that names of the same things are with the Gods different from those that subsist in the opinion of men:*

'Xanthus by Gods, by men Scamander call'd.' [Iliad xx v 74].

...For as the knowledge of the Gods is different from that of partial souls...since divine names unfold the whole essence of the things named. Platon, therefore, knowing that this pre-existed in the world, omits the divine and ineffable name itself." (Proklus Commentary on Platon Timaios 28b).

As it is written:

"*How that he was caught up into paradise, and heard ineffable words, which it is not lawful for a man to utter.*" (2nd Letter to Corinthians 12:4).

As above, so below as it is written:

"*'Come, gaze upon the works of Alohim, what שמות (feats) He put on Earth.' (Sefer Tehillim 46:9).*

Do not read שמות (feats) but שמת (names). This corresponds to what Rab ḫiyya said 'Corresponding to Heaven, the Blessed Holy One fashioned on Earth. In Heaven there are holy names, on Earth there are holy names." (Sefer HaZohar Midrash HaNelam 2:5a).

Theurgic names to accomplish great feats, whose *works are of Alohim*! The Baal HaShem will more than know and understand!

19:15 ~ "And out of his mouth goeth a sharp SWORD, that with it he should smite the goyim: and he shall rule them with a rod of iron: and he treadeth the winepress of the fierceness and wrath of El Shaddai."

In this chapter, one is given many metonyms for Mashiaḫ. These are *WORD of HaAlohim*, *SWORD*, *NAAMAN* (The FAITHFUL ONE), and *EMETH* (TRUTH). Sefer HaZohar and Philon, the great Jewish epopt, are all in perfect agreement en passim. The Adept will more than know and understand. Yet, I will leave the reader with one proof and confirmation, along with other metonyms, from The SOURCE himself who saith:

"...אנכי *(I AM) [the]* אמת *(TRUTH),* חיים *(LIFE), [and]* דרך *(WAY).*" (Book of Yoɧanan 14:6).

As it was originally written in the original ancient Hebrew scroll. Esoterically and subliminally, through the arcane principle of Notarikon, telling us that he is אחד (The ONE).

It is also written:

"*Think not that I am come to send peace on Earth: I came not to send peace, but a SWORD.*" (Sefer Mattityahu 10:34).

"*...He [HaMashiaɧ] shall consume all the goyim his enemies...*" (Sefer Bamidbar 24:8).

"*For the day of* יהוה *is near, a day of cloud; it shall be the end of the goyim*" (LXX Yeɧezkeyl 30:3).

Prythee understand silly and foolish Christians and goyim.

19:19 ~ "And I saw the beast, and the kings of the earth, and their armies, gathered together to make war against him that sat on the horse, and against his army."

This will be a marvelous sight to behold! Actually, to much of the world, it will actually appear to be like that of a hostile Alien Invasion. The darkened Satanists have been covertly employing predictive programming through numerous media to deceive the world into believing this great delusion. Soon they will unite the world for the purposes of defeating this great Alien Invasion which is none other than the return of Mashiaɧ and his angels. This was intimated during a speech at the Luciferian United Nations by former American president Ronald Reagan:

"*Perhaps we need some outside, universal threat to make us recognize this common bond. I occasionally think how quickly our differences worldwide would vanish if we were facing an alien threat from outside of this world.*"

At this time, most of the world will have a great hatred towards Adonay, like a rebellious son hating his father for imposing rules and punishing him.

20:3 ~ "And cast him into the bottomless pit, and shut him up, and set a seal upon him, that he should deceive the nations no more, till the thousand years should be fulfilled: and after that he must be loosed a little season."

This is all in accord with the primordial esoteric doctrines of the knowledge and wisdom of Time and the Universe. As stated and proved in my first Treatise, Time is a superimposition of numerous cycles. Two of the larger cycles are the 8,000 year cycle or the Great Shmittah Cycle and the 50,000 year cycle or the Great Yobel Cycle; the number 7 and 50 being their archetype. The 8,000 year cycle is really 7,000 years with the addition of 1,000 years. The 1,000 years always represent the Golden Age within each Great Shmitttah Cycle. Additionally, this Age is always contained in two Great Shmittah Cycles, simultaneously being the last 1,000 years of the former, while the first of the latter. This, of course, creates seven exact Great Shmittah Cycles in one Great Yobel Cycle.

In this case, these 1,000 years concurrently represent the last 1,000 years of this Aeon and the beginning of the next Aeon. Being the Golden Age, it is no surprise that HaSatan must be restrained. Then, *he is loosened out of his prison* for 7,000 years. All progressing according to the revolutions and harmonics of the Universe.

20:4-6 ~ "And I saw thrones, and they sat upon them, and judgment was given unto them: and I saw the souls of them that were beheaded for the witness of YESHUAH, and for the WORD of Alohim, and which had not worshipped the beast, neither his image, neither

had received his mark upon their foreheads, or in their hands; and they lived and reigned with HaMashiaḫ a thousand years. But the rest of the dead lived not again until the thousand years were finished. This is the first resurrection. Blessed and holy is he that hath part in the first resurrection: on such the second death hath no power, but they shall be Kohanim of Alohim and of HaMashiaḫ …"

It seems as if they verse intimates that ONLY the holy martyrs of the last generation of this Aeon will reign as Alohim with Mashiaḫ in the Garden of Eden. Also, just as there are two deaths, so likewise there are two resurrections. It then seems appropriate to ask what is the difference between these two resurrections?

The key to the answer lies in the verses. The second death has no application to those of the first resurrection. Now, the second death is nothing less than spiritual annihilation as already proven. These spirits are inferior and not made in the image of Alohim. Otherwise, by definition and by his essence, Alohim would not be able to destroy his own image! This is why no Israelite, being his children, and his own genera, that of HaAlohim, may be destroyed or partake of the second death as it is written:

"*All of thy people are righteous…*" (Sefer Yeshayahu 60:21).

Which prompted the great Qabbalist Shaul, knowing these great mysteries and secrets, to write:

"*And so all of Israel shall be saved: as it is written, 'There shall come out of Tziyyon the Deliverer, and shall turn away ungodliness from Yaqob' [Sefer Yeshayahu 45:17].*" (Romans 11:26).

As it is also written:

"*And he shall redeem Israel from all his iniquities.*" (Sefer Tehillim 130:8).

It does not say Israel and the goyim! For there are two goyim. Those that are crypto-Israelites, who are ignorant of their bloodline viz. Christians. And those who are not Israelite. This is the great mystery that only very initiated saints understand like Shaul. The Adept will know and understand.

Now, at this point, it should be readily comprehended that there are very great arcana behind these two resurrections. If the second death has no application to the first resurrection, then it logically follows that it does to the second resurrection! This is what separates or distinguishes both resurrections. Why and how could that be? Very simply, those of the first resurrection will inhabit the Golden Age. However, those of the second resurrection are not given this opportunity. Ergo, they will reside in the other inferior part of the next Aeon viz. the other 7,000 years. More relevantly, by nature and essence, the second death only applies to those who have tasted the first death! Ergo, it logically follows that those of the second resurrection must be liable to the first death. And there is the revelation! The second resurrection alludes to reincarnation in a second body in the next Aeon. And so we have one more manifest proof of many for the esoteric doctrine of metempsychosis.

Anent the general resurrection, it is written:

"*For* יהוה *himself shall descend from heaven with a shout, with the voice of The Arch-Angel, and with the trump of Alohim: and the dead in Mashiaḫ shall rise first:*
Then we which are alive and remain shall be caught up together with them in the clouds, to meet יהוה *in the air: and so shall we ever be with* יהוה." (1 Thessalonians 14:16-17).

Thus, in the initial stages of the general resurrection, all of the righteous ascend. However, there are two subsets or laws that govern the general resurrection. Those who partake of the first subset or resurrection are privileged to continue to stay on Earth to inhabit the Golden Age with יהוה. The second law or resurrection pertains to those who are not permitted to stay on Earth and inhabit the Golden Age. These, upon being resurrected, return to Heaven with יהוה

where according to certain laws and judgments return to Earth at appointed fixed times as *the rest of the dead lived not again [on Earth] until the thousand years were finished* as it is likewise written:

"*Of these souls some, such as have earthward tendencies and material tastes descend to be fast bound in mortal bodies, **while others ascend being selected for return according to the numbers and periods determined by nature**.*" (Philon On Dreams I 138).

Because how can those of the second resurrection, being resurrected which is reanimation and living again, be said not to live again? Precisely, the matter is as I have written. And yes יהוה can be simultaneously on Earth and Heaven as he is HaAlohim! This is a great mystery and Arcanum only understood by the Highest Initiates!!! Incorporeal and corporeal life are two separate matters. Put another way, life in Heaven and on Earth are two separate matters. Even renowned Masters of Israel do not know this as it is written:

"*And Yeshuah answered and said unto him: Are thou a Master of Israel and knowest not these things?... And no man hath ascended up to heaven, but he that came down from heaven, even the Son of Man which is in heaven.*" (Book of Yoḫanan 3:10-13).

Read it carefully and meditate and you will understand. How can Yeshuah the *Son of Man* be simultaneously on Heaven and Earth!!!??? This alludes to one of the highest Arcana dealing with the Upper Spirit. This is all I will say for much has been revealed!

And no, obviously the *resurrection of the judgment* or damned is in no way being referenced as it is entirely separate!

The Garden of Eden is the habitation of Alohim and their genera. As such, those that partake of the first resurrection are elevated to Alohim as it is written:

"*I have said, Ye are Alohim; and all of you are children of Elyon.*" (Sefer Tehillim 82:6).

Just as Rabbi said:

"*Neither can they die any more: for they are equal unto the angels; and are the children of Alohim, being the children of the resurrection.*" (Luke 20:36).

Ergo, the Golden Ages, likened unto the Garden of Eden, of the Aeons are distinct from the other part of the Aeon. They are inhabited by both men and HaAlohim as well as Alohim. The other part of the Aeon, however, is only inhabited by men.

20:8 ~ "And shall go out to deceive the nations which are in the four quarters of the earth which are Gog and Magog, to gather them together to battle: the number of whom is as the sand of the sea."

This is a very interesting and curious verse as I shall now relate. Now, the first relevant reference to Gog is in an oracle in HaTorah that is partially corrupted in the Masoretic text. So we must look to the superior LXX in this case for the proper analysis. First, I provide the only full translation given by our most ancient initiated Hebrew Hierophant:

"*There shall come forth from you one day a man and he shall rule over many goyim, and his kingdom spreading every day shall be exalted Gog (on high)...*" (Philon Mushah I 290 citing Sefer Bamidbar 24:7).

The Hebrew word *Gog* signifies '*top*', '*roof*', or '*high*'. Ergo, the correct translation given by Philon. Moreover, I shall also provide another telestic interpretation provided by the LXX's pointing to the underlying Hebrew vorlage:

"*...and the kingdom of Gog shall be exalted and his kingdom shall be increased.*" (Sefer Bamidbar 24:7).

So, now we have a concurrent increase of two opposing governments. The children of HaMashiaђ versus the children of HaSatan. The proof is easily recorded in the History of the past 2,000 years!

Gog is the name of one of the leading spiritual divine princes or gods of the 7 in the Qlippothic godhead as it is written:

"*...the prince of Ros (or chief prince or ROSiyah [Russia in Russian])...*" (Sefer Yeђezkeyl 38:2).

He is so powerful that he lords over many of the other 70 archons in the Satanic godhead. This is because his creates a confederacy full of many goyim as it is written of him:

"*...and many goyim shall be with you.*" (Ibid. verse 6).

"*...assembled from many goyim.*" (Ibid. verse 8).

"*...and many goyim with you...*" (Ibid. verse15).

Thus, it is evident that mystically, Gog is a powerful god over many evil goyim, while Magog is the designation given to these people. Magog is also Hebrew for *from Gog*, indicating that these goyim are under his control. Hence, the equation of Gog and Magog to the evil goyim should now be readily apprehended in the verse supra. Specifically, that the evil goyim in *the four wings of the Earth* are Magog. And he shall gather them, that is Gog and Magog, or the evil goyim in *the four wings of the Earth* and their leader against his holy Saints.

Now, for the proof and the interesting part. Behold! It is written:

"*At the end of days it shall be, and I will lead you up against my land...*" (Ibid. verse 16).

"*And it will be on that day, I will give to Gog a noteworthy place as a tomb in Israel...and they shall bury there Gog and all his multitude and they shall call it the Valley of Hamon-Gog (the multitude of Gog).*" (Ibid. 39:11-12).

Yet, we are told of another war involving Gog and Magog in the next Aeon after the Golden Age! So that either there is a contradiction or Gog has reincarnated! But, it is as I have explicated. Gog refers to the spiritual archon of Magog. Currently, we are less than half a generation away from the war of Gog and Magog; given that we are in the last days. Additionally, we are also told of that war recurring about 8,000 thousand years from now; the last days of the next Aeon! Which is proof of the symbolic representations of Gog and Magog just given. Amen, more proof of what is written:

"*The thing that hath been, it is that which shall be; and that which is done is that which shall be done: and there is no new thing under the sun.*" (Ecclesiastes 1:9)

Ergo, the end of every Aeon is marked by the war of Gog and Magog. And the beginning of every Aeon is marked by a Golden Age of 1,000 years. All part of the Revolution of the Aeons and Souls.

20:13 ~ "...and Death and Sheol delivered up the dead which were in them..."

Again, as it is written:

"*יהוה killeth, and maketh alive: he bringeth down to Sheol, and bringeth up.*" (Shamuel Alef 2:6).

21:1 ~ "And I saw a new Heaven and a new Earth: for the first Heaven and the first Earth were passed away; and there was no more sea."

As it is written:

“*These are the generations/births of the Heavens and of the Earth when they were created...*” (Sefer Breyshith 2:4).

“*For, behold, I create new Heavens and a new Earth: and the former shall not be remembered, nor come into mind.*” (Sefer Yeshayahu 65:17).

Which prompted the ancient Israeli Qabbalists to veraciously teach:

“*The Holy One blessed be he! created and destroyed several aeons/worlds before the present one was made...*” (Ibid. 3:61b).

And there is a very profound, very esoteric mystery in the first line of HaTorah. The first two strings may be split and read as follows:

“ ‘ברא *(Aramaic for ‘The SON’])* שית *(Aramaic for ‘sixth’)* ברא *(Hebrew for ‘He created’)’* (Sefer Breyshith 1:1)

Which reads: *He created the sixth son*. Mystery of why Adam was created on the sixth day. Because there were 5 prototypes or versions before him. Because there were 5 Aeons before him. Evidently this implies five previous destructions! This is a very great Arcanum! As it is written:

“*There have been and there will be many and divers destructions of mankind, of which the greatest are by fire and water, and lesser ones by countless other means...for, in the first place, you remember but one deluge, though many had occurred previously...*” (Platon Timaios 22c-23b)

“*The Gematria of* בראשית *is equivalent to* שש סדרים *(six orders) [which is 913]...*”(Baal HaTurim Commentary to Sefer Breyshith 1:1).

These six orders represent the 5 Aeons before us plus the current Aeon we inhabit. Another telestic interpretation: the sixth son is in reference to the sixth pillar of the seven pillars or Lower 7th Sfiroth. Mystery of:

"*...He became a father according to his form and according to his image and named his name שית (Aramaic: Six).*" (LXX Sefer Breyshith 5:3).

This is of course Mashiaĥ who is in the image of the 6th Divine Son who is TZADDIQ. Mystery of the *seven spirits* or emanations above him; five elder brothers plus his mother and father. And this too is another great Arcanum!

Another interpretation:

"ברא *(Aramaic for 'The SON'])* שית *(Aramaic for 'six')*" (Sefer Breyshith 1:1).

Or:

"*The Son is* ו *(Gematira of 6).*" (Ibid.).

As it is written:

"ו who is The Son of YAH." (Sefer Tiqquney HaZohar 13:2).

And so Yoĥanan is in full accord with ancient esoteric veracious doctrines. A new generation of the Heavens and the Earth as HaTorah teaches. The Earth must be judged for the iniquity of Adam or mankind. The Heavens for the iniquity of its host (the stars and the luminaries) as it is written:

"*And it shall come to pass, in that day, that* יהוה *shall punish the Host of the High Heaven on high. And they shall be gathered together, as prisoners are gathered in the prison, and shall be shut up in the fortress...*" (LXX Sefer Yeshayahu 24:21).

Again, all part of the revolution of the Aeons and Souls. The Blessed Holy One, blessed is He, is like the Architect or Potter on the wheel, spinning and spinning the circle.

21:2 ~ "And I Yoђanan saw the holy city, new YERUSHALEM, coming down from Alohim out of Heaven, prepared as the BRIDE adorned for her Husband.

Lo! Exactly as it is written in our ancient concealed midrashim:

"*The Blessed Holy One is destined to renew this world, to rebuild Yerushalem and lower her down fully built from on high, an indestructible edifice!*" (Sefer HaZohar Midrash HaNelam 1:114b).

Another interpretation. This is obviously none other than NOђAH or SHEђINAH. For YERUSHALEM is a code word for Her.

21:3 ~ "And I heard a great voice out of Heaven saying, Behold, the Sukkah (tabernacle) of Alohim is with men, and he will dwell with them, and they shall be his people, and Alohim himself shall be with them, and be their Alohim."

The true meaning and significance behind the Feast of Sukkoth or Tabernacles. For what else is this feast than preparation for this day and Age spoken of here.

21:9-10 ~ "Come hither, I will shew thee the BRIDE, the LAMAB'S wife. And he carried me away in the spirit to a great and high mountain, and shewed me that great city, the holy YERUSHALEM, descending out of Heaven from Alohim."

In these verses as well as the subsequent, he is describing NOђAH, veiled through her symbols. For by YERUSHALEM, he signifies NOђAH. We know that *mountain* is a code word for an Al or Emanation. Her appearance is linked with gemstones like that of sapphire and *like a jasper stone clear as crystal* as it is written:

"*And they saw Elohey Yisrael: and there was under his feet as it were a paved work of crystal diamond (white sapphire/precious stone) ...*" (Sefer Shmoth 24:10).

Under his feet. Precisely. Representing the 10th Divine Emanation. Her *twelve gates* represent the 12 divine elders or entities below her. These gates are divided into four regions viz. *east*, to represent the four ƙerubim who support her. Her dimensions are given in ratios or proportions of her attributes; the number 12 viz. *144 and 12,000.*

21:21 ~ "And the twelve gates were twelve pearls/gemstones; every several gate was of one pearl/gemstone: and the street of the city was pure gold, as it were transparent glass."

As it is written:

"*And the gates of YERUSHALEM will be built with sapphires and emerald and all your walls with precious stones. The towers of YERUSHALEM will be built with gold and their battlements with pure gold. The streets of YERUSHALEM will be paved with ruby and stone of Ofir.*" (LXX Sefer Tobiyahu 13:16-18).

And of our holy Heavenly Mother, blessed is She, it is likewise written:

"*...The Queen stood at your right hand in gold woven clothing, decked out in many colors.*" (LXX Sefer Tehillim 44:10).

"*Of the Daughter of the King...decked out with golden tassels in many colors.*" (Ibid. verse 14).

Not to be confused with Lillith of whom it is written:

"*...that was clothed in fine linen, and purple, and scarlet, and decked with gold, and precious stones, and pearls!*" (Book of the Apocalypse 18:16).

She is just a perverse imitation of the Blessed Holy One, blessed is She.

21:27 ~ "And there shall in no wise enter into it any thing that defileth, neither whatsoever worketh abomination, or maketh a lie: but they which are written in the Lamb's book of life."

What is being described here as well is the lowest level in the Heavens of the Heavens. For HaAlohim are not just Alohim but also habitations or great palaces. Each one of HaAlohim also represent a level of the Heavens. YERUSHALEM, or NOȞAH, also represents the 10th level of the Heavens. This is why she also known as The SEA. For the SEA is a vast habitation. For remember, by definition, an El is everywhere! She is the gateway or portal to the higher dimensions. Amen, amen, the Epopt will know and understand.

22:1 ~ "And he shewed me a pure river of water of LIFE, clear as crystal, proceeding out of the throne of HaAlohim and of the LAMB."

As it is written:

"*And a river went out of EDEN to water the garden; and from thence it was parted, and became into four heads.*" (Sefer Breyshith 2:10).

What is being described here are the beginning of further emanations from Lower ȞOȞMAH. For from Sefer HaZohar, we know that rivers of water represent the channeling and flow of the Emanations. From these two verses we may then derive part of the ancient esoteric ȞOȞMAH as it is written:

"*'A river', it says, 'issues forth from EDEN to water the garden' [Ibid.]*

...This issues forth out of EDEN, the ḫOḫMAH of Alohim, and this is the LOGOS of Alohim." (Philon Allegorical Interpretation I 64-65).

"ברא *(He created [Aramaic for The SON])* בראשית *(BREYSHITH)" [Sefer Breyshith 1:1]*

'BeReyshith (With BEGINNING)' is an utterance, 'He created', half an utterance. Father and Son, concealed and revealed. Upper EDEN, concealed and hidden. Lower EDEN, departing on its journeys..." (Sefer HaZohar Sifra di-Tzeniuta [Book of the Concealed] 2:178b).

So, EDEN represents the *throne of Alohim*, or Upper ḫOḫMAH, Mother and Father as one. The river represents Lower ḫOḫMAH, Son and Daughter as one. Yes, ye are beginning to comprehend these supernal matters.

22:2 ~ "In the midst of the street of it, and on either side of the river, was there the TREE of LIFE, which bare twelve manner of fruits, and yielded her fruit every month: and the leaves of the tree were for the healing of the nations."

The TREE of LIFE is Upper ḫOḫMAH. The twelve fruits represent the 12 Divine Elders. The leaves are the angels of Alohim.

22:4 ~ "*And they shall see his face; and his name shall be in their foreheads.*"

The true reason behind the statute of the wearing of Tefillin on our foreheads by us Yehudim. By doing so, we imitate and look forward to this day!

22:17 ~ "*And the SPIRIT and the BRIDE say, Come. And let him that heareth say, Come. And let him that is athirst come. And whosoever will, let him take the water of life freely.*"

The RUAĦ HAKEDUSHAH (The HOLY SPIRIT), or BRIDE imploring us to her bosom. I long to return to the divine breasts of my Heavenly Mother!

First Gate to Hadad
(The Orchard/Paradise):
Esoteric Tosefta (Addendum)

The Bitten Pomegranate

Once, over the course of many days I was studying and meditating on what little I knew of metempsychosis. I knew that Great Teaching of the ancient Mashħilim, that everything is encoded in HaTorah! That HaTorah is nothing more than a collection of divine parables. I knew that the complete esoteric doctrines of metempsychosis were in the WORD. So I prayed to HaAlohim that he would give me the sight to see the mysteries behind the transmigration of souls. One day, while reciting Tehillim 46:

"על עלמות שיר *(A song upon hidden matters [or virgins])*" (verse 1).

And the SHMA before bed, suddenly, the blessed holy virgin SARAH, blessed is She, appeared to me in all her beauty and glory!

Me: … I know of the great mysteries behind the transmigrations of HaMashiaħ in HaTorah. But what of the pious of Yisrael, his children who are not HaAlohim?

SARAH: My blessed beloved son, you should know this great mystery. Rabbeinu (Our LORD) spoke and alluded to it when he spoke of Yonah and that Great Fish who is called Lewiyathan.

Me: I see. I know that Yonah represented HaMashiaħ and the Great Fish or *Serpent of the SEA* represented Sheol as it is written:

"*For as Yonah was three days and three nights in the whale's belly; so shall the Son of man be three days and three nights in the heart of the earth.*" (Sefer Mattityahu 12:40).

"*So is this great and wide SEA…There go the ships: there is that Lewiyathan…*" (Sefer Tehillim 104:25-26).

SARAH: But there is more. Sections that you are blind too. But, I shall reveal to you the missing holes to complete the picture found in that ancient holy sefer.

Why must every Yisraeli male make pilgrimage to Tziyyon (פעמים שלוש) 3 times a year? What is the great secret or mystery behind this?

Me: I don't know. Please tell me!

SARAH: Recall what the ancient sages taught from the holy scriptures:

"*Rab Yirmeyah ben Elazar said:*

'Geyhinnom has 3 gates…1 in Yerushalem as it is said:

'…declares יהוה, whose Fire is in Tziyyon, his Furnace in Yerushalem.' (Sefer Yeshayahu 31:9).

'This is the opening of Geyhinnom'." (Talmud Babli Tractate Erubin 19a).

"*There is a gate beneath Tziyyon…beneath The Holy Temple…a subterranean fire…when holy male circumcised Yisraelites stand above it, they submerge that fire to the great depth – fire of Sheol.*" (Sefer Zohar ђadash The Concealed Midrash 79b).

Lo! It is written:

"*And the WORD of יהוה came unto Yonah.. saying... Arise, go to Ninweh, that great city, and cry against it; for their wickedness is come up before me.*" (Sefer Yonah 1:1-2).

El telling the spirit Yonah to leave The Heavens to go to Ninweh, the evil world just as *he sent forth Adam* and Abraham.

"*But Yonah rose up to flee unto Tharshish from the presence of יהוה, and went down to Yoppeh; and he found a ship...and went down into it, to go with them unto Tharshish from the presence of יהוה.*" (Ibid. 3).

His spirit goes into the ship, the body, descending into vanity, Yoppeh (pleasure or beauty), which is away from the straight path of Adonay.

"*But יהוה sent out a great wind into the sea, and there was a mighty tempest in the sea, so that the ship was like to be broken.*" (Ibid. 4).

The body being rocked and tossed to and fro by the evil impulse as it is written:

"*And if SHEḫINAH is not there, a whirlwind (a troubling wind/spirit) is there, which agitates the body of Adam. It is written about it:*

'and the ship was considered broken.' (Ibid.).

Which is the body of the ship." (Sefer Tiqquney HaZohar 35:2).

"*...But Yonah was gone down into the sides of the ship; and he lay, and was fast asleep.*" (Ibid. 5).

Yonah being spiritually asleep to righteousness as the spirit is weakened by the body.

"*So they took up Yonah, and cast him forth into the sea: and the sea ceased from her raging.*" (Ibid. 15).

The spirit leaving the body, death, now in peace from the evil impulse and its dominion and stronghold.

"*And Yonah was in the belly of the fish three days and three nights.*" (Ibid. 17).

Lewiyathan, the fish monster in the SEA, prince of Sheol, the belly of the Earth. There for 3 days of Adonay which is 3000 years!!! All proof found in the next chapter, a psalm of deliverance from Sheol for the people of Yisrael!

"*And יהוה spake unto the Fish, and it vomited out Yonah upon the dry land.*" (Ibid. 2:10).

Adonay answering his prayer and delivering the spirit from Sheol into a new body.

"*And the WORD of יהוה came to Yonah a second time saying, 'Arise and go to Ninweh...*" (Ibid. 3:1-2).

Mystery of the matter. A second incarnation, a second chance to redeem his soul after being delivered from Sheol! Exactly as it is written:

"*Yes, **his soul drew near to death, and his life was in Sheol**. If there be 1000 death-bearing angels, not one of them shall wound him; if he purpose with his heart to repent to יהוה and declare to a person his own fault and reveal his folly. He will provide support...and **renew his body** like paint does a wall...Deliver my soul so that it may not go to corruption...**Look! EL works all these things** פעמים שלוש **(3 times [or 2 or 3 times]) with a mighty man**.*" (Sefer Yob 33:22-29)

A parable my young beloved son:

"*Here one must contemplate! The craftsman who extracts silver from the source of the Earth, what does he do? At first he inserts it within a raging fire until the slime of the Earth is completely removed, leaving silver though not unadulterated silver. What does he do afterward? He inserts it in fire as at fist and extracts the dross as is said*

'Remove the dross from the silver...' (Book of Proverbs 25:4).

Then it is pure silver without intermingling." (Sefer HaZohar Midrash HaNelam 1:116a).

Another parable:

"*What is this like? A person planted a vineyard and hoped to grow grapes, but instead, sour grapes grew. He saw that his planting and harvest were not successful so he tore it out. He cleansed out the sour grape vines and planted it again.*" (Sefer HaBahir 134 [195]).

For it is written that Alohim planted trees in the Garden as it is written:

"...כי האדם עץ *(for HaAdam is a tree)...*" (Sefer Debarim 20:19).

Ergo, mankind is the divine plant of Alohim. And many of these divine plants are replanted or reincarnated as many times as needed. And Yisrael is his vineyard. Yet, the most explicit proof is found in our grandiloquent esoteric translation of that infamous verse in HaTorah:

"*And it shall be that the firstborn whom she beareth, on account thereof (or from thence or through there), his dead brother shall arise...*" (Sefer Debarim 25:6).

And so 3 times you must go to Tziyyon to subdue the fires of Geyhinnom below, tied to the 3 chances or deliverances from Sheol a holy man obtains in total if he so keeps the yearly holy pilgrimages. And there are greater and more sublime revelations concerning this topic. But, this suffices for now.

Me: If I only came into this world to hear the elucidation of this mystery, it would more than suffice!!! Amen, amen, Adonay is extremely loving and compassionate, full of infinities of mercy and loving-kindness!!! As it is written:

"*He has not even tried me commensurate with my sin!!*" (Ibid. 27).

Halleluyah!!! I can't wait to return to suckle from thy divine breasts once again my Holy Blessed Mother! For it is better than the merry gluhwein you have just fed me.

The Bitten Fig

Once, I was praying and meditating over the psalm:

"*Regarding completion, secrets of The Son...*" (Sefer Tehillim 9:1)

Suddenly, Miȟael bore me on his wings and I was taken to Heaven. I saw Heaven divided into 3 regions, each subdivided into infinite levels. There was the Outer Court, the Inner Court, and the Holy of Holies. I instantly noticed how the overwhelming proportion of Christians were in the Outer and Inner Court. Not surprising to me, being a Jew, I also noticed how the Holy of Holies was almost solely comprised of Jews. So I asked Miȟael for understanding on the divisions and their numbers.

Me: Why are there hardly any Christians in the Holy of Holies?

MIȞAEL: LO! It is written:

"*What then is the superiority of the Jew?...Much in every way!!! First Indeed [are they]!!! For they were entrusted with the oracles of Alohim!*" (Letter to the Romans 3:1-2).

Shaul, being an initiated Jew, knew this very well as so do you. You see, Christianity was, lamentably, subverted within one generation after the departure of The Faithful Shepherd!

Suddenly tears began to roll down the eyes of the Blessed Holy One, Blessed be He for his children.

Me: How did this come about?

MIȞAEL: The way by which is came about is very convoluted and would take a long time to explain in words. But it was all brought about through the Evil One and his attendants. However, I will simplify the subversion for thee. It all amounts to one major Error! You see, Abraham represents the archetype of every Goy who is grafted into the Holy Vine, or more properly regrafted. He represents the process of initiation into the holy mysteries and of supernal consummation. The first step or entrance begins with Faith which is reckoned as Righteousness. This is the first gate into the Holy Vineyard. And every Christian easily enters this gate through faith in HaMashiaḫ. Yet, after this, are higher gates, the mitzwoth of HaTorah or HaBrith. It is to be a gradual progression beginning with the covenant of circumcision; progressing into the higher mystical statutes. For the covenant of circumcision is the first mitzwah observed by every Yisraeli male. Once all 611 mitzwoth are attained, the gematria of Torah and Brith, then and only then does supernal and holy consummation take place. Thus, meriting the change of name or glory. All this is represented by Abraham the archetype for the goy coming to Alohim. Unfortunately and poignantly, over 99% of Christians never get past Gate 1! Note that Abraham does not reach the first covenant or mitzwah of circumcision until the midpoint of his life. This is the expectation put upon the Goy who is to enter. And he does not attain the fullness of HaTorah until close to the end of his life. Again, this is the expectation of the Goy. Ergo, Abraham's progression into the Covenant stands as a benchmark for the Goyim. So it should be readily apparent how horribly the Christians have failed and come short! The Jews on the other hand, are fully initiated and close to the end of supernal consummation. Moreover, those who are Adepts and beyond know The Son and the many names and titles by which he goes by. For I have been invoked by many Jewish Adepts, well-versed in the mystic arts, under many theurgic names such as Metatron, Yahuel, and even Miḫael! For according to the spiritual mystic sciences, names are just a means to the divine entity by representing their essence. Ergo, it is the Jewish Adepts that have a better apprehension and comprehension of HaMashiaḫ then do the Christians. For the Christians have lamentably perverted the true image of HaMashiaḫ and his teachings regarding HaTorah! For how can they know that which they have never attained nor safeguarded!? It is for this reason that they are the lowest in the Kingdom as it is written:

"*Whosoever therefore shall break one of these least commandments, and shall teach men so, he shall be called the least in the Kingdom of Heaven: but whosoever shall do and teach them, the same shall be called great in the Kingdom of Heaven.*" (Sefer Mattityahu 5:19).

As you know, there are 611 mitzwoth. Keeping 10 and rejecting and breaking the others suffices! For this reason, my beloved son, you will be very great in the Kingdom of Heaven!

Suddenly, Kefa the Chief Disciple of Rabbi appeared next to Miɧael.

KEFA: Neither, therefore, are the Jews condemned on account of their ignorance of Yeshuah, by reason of Him who has concealed Him, if, doing the things commanded by Mushah, they do not hate Him whom they do not know. Neither are those from among the goyim condemned, who know not Mushah on account of Him who has concealed him, provided that these also, doing the things spoken by Yeshuah, do not hate Him whom they do not know. And some will not be profited by calling the teachers lords, but not doing the works of servants. For on this account our Yeshuah Himself said to one who often called Him Adoni, but did none of the things which He prescribed, "Why call ye me Adoni, Adoni, and do not the things which I say?" For it is not saying that will profit any one, but doing. For Mushah and Yeshuah are one and the same Teacher! Two sides of the same coin if you may.

Then Miɧael shapeshifted into Metatron and said:

"I will now tell you a very great secret pertaining to the superiority of Judaism, the receptacle of the ancient Israelite theosophy as it is written:

"*What then is the superiority of the Jew?....Much in every way for first indeed they were entrusted with the oracles of Alohim.*" (Book to the Romans 3:1).

Long, long ago as you know, The 10 Tribes of Yisrael corrupted and perverted their theosophy by which only their brethren, The House of Yehudah preserved. Still with a foundation in it, they nevertheless changed the priesthood, holy festivals, and the location where ADONAY put his name, namely Yerushalem to Bethel. Their self-acclaimed superiority to their Jewish brethren was quickly confuted with their destruction and exile! Likewise with the parable of the Samaritan woman who asked Yeshua HaMashiaḫ:

"*Our fathers worshipped in this mountain; and ye say, that in Jerusalem is the place where men ought to worship?*" (Sefer Yoḫanan 4:20).

He replied back:

"*Ye worship ye know not what: we know what we worship: for salvation is of the Jews.*" (Ibid. verse 22).

Amen! Many of these Samaritans were the ancient bethren to the Jews, the lost 10 tribes. Their religion was based and rooted in the ancient theosophy of Israel like the Jews. They for the most part shared the same bible and yet both religions represented by their two mountains of worship were in opposition. Does this remind of you anything?

I quickly replied:

"Oh ADONAY (My Lords)!"

Amen, these are the ancient archetypes to modern day Christianity and Judaism. And as you already know, it is more than evident who will be in for a very rude and shocking awakening!

Then Metatron shapeshifted into Yeshua.

Yeshua: This is the great secret that the Christians, my beloved children, do not understand. For me to live in someone is for that individual to become me or like me. For I am their Father, their archetype, and so as I observed HaTorah here on Earth, while I was on Earth, setting the example and benchmark, so shall they! For how can they say that I live in them when they do not keep HaTorah as I did! For to truly walk in the Spirit is to transcend HaTorah. That is, when you walk in the Spirit you are keeping and fulfilling HaTorah perfectly as I did when I was on Earth. If so, then, how then can

HaTorah have application to you! For just as Evil has no application to one who cannot feel pain or suffering, so a Torah has no application to one who is sinless by keeping it perfectly! For by definition, a Torah serves the purpose to force a person into complete subjection into its mitzwoth. But a holy saint who is already in complete observance to all the mitzwoth is no longer in need of Torah! Amen, amen, HaTorah only rules over them that are not in perfect subjection to it! But I rule over them who are in complete perfect subjection to it thus walking in the Spirit as did I! This is the great mystery that the Apostle Shaul attempted to convey in his writings that they unfortunately misinterpreted! But can a baby understand a full mature adult?

Suddenly, I was taken to the Gates of Heaven where I beheld numerous Christians entering. As each one waited to enter the Gates, the Ben HaQol exclaimed:

“"Why call ye me Adonay, Adonay, and did not the things which I said, taught, and fulfilled in keeping HaTorah?”

Then I would see many tears run down the Christians for their ignorance. But because they had the Faith, they were all allowed to enter on account of being The Blessed Holy One’s children and his great love and compassion for them. But many were not allowed in the inner court and practically none made into the holy of holies!

The Bitten Etrog

Once, I was praying and meditating over the holy oracular rebuke:

"*Ye took up the tabernacle of Moloђ and Kiyyun (Saturn) the star of the god of ye, the images which you made for ye.*" (Sefer Amos 5:26).

Suddenly, I astrally projected over the star Saturn and saw what could only be described as an abode of Samael. It was black and dark and full of satanic gothic structures based on entropy or chaos. Then the Spirits of Knowledge, Wisdom, and Understanding penetrated my heart.

And I understood that the modern Hebrew name for the star Saturn, שבתי (Shabbatai) was a corruption. For its true ancient name is Kiyyun. This was partly based on ignornant goyim speaking on matters way above their comprehension such as the ancient Roman historian who wrote:

"*We are told that the 7th day was set aside for rest because this marked the end of their toils...others say that this is a mark of respect for Saturn...*" (Tacitus Histories Book 5 § 4).

And so the uninitiated and ignorant ancient Rabbanan are responsible for the spurious and unnecessary renaming of Saturn after the second temple period. Based on this corruption, many ignorant Rabbanan equated the star with שבת (Shabbath).

Another great problem is the many Jewish Qabbalists who are not fully initiated and who hold very erroneous beliefs despite high initiation. Rab Abraham ben Ezra is one perfect example. For he writes in one of his astrological treatises:

"*Saturn...of the nations, in his share are the...Jews...*" (Reyshith Hoђmah Chapter 4).

Oh, what blasphemy and stupidity!!! How could a Baal HaTorah and polymath such as him believe this utter nonsense is utterly beyond me! There has been among the Jewish Qabbalists an inferior or secondary elite that teaches and holds on to spurious doctrines. Lamentably, much of the true esoteric and primeval astrology has been lost or corrupted.

Nevertheless, allow me to completely shut down and refute this very blasphemous teaching by Abenezra. Lo! It is written:

"*There is no mazal (celestial flux) over Yisrael.*" (Talmud Babli Tractate Shabbath 156A).

The folio supra provides many satisfactory proofs. But the seal is in HaTorah:

"*And lest thou lift up thine eyes unto heaven, and when thou seest the sun, and the moon, and the stars, even all the host of heaven, shouldest be driven to worship them, and serve them, which the יהוה thy Alohim hath divided/apportioned unto all nations under the whole heaven.*" (Sefer Debarim 4:19).

Thus, the entire goyim are under the influence of The Host of Heaven. Because:

"*For the portion of יהוה is his people; Yaqob is the lot/portion of his inheritance.*" (LXX Ibid. 32:8-9).

Ergo, Yisrael is unique in that is directly ruled over by HaAlohim whereas the goyim are NOT, and thus ruled over by The Host of Heaven!

Now, Qabbalists like Abenezra erroneously believe that on a primary basis, the Jews are ruled over by certain constellations and stars. But, when they are Torah observant, these powers are then superseded by HaAlohim! Actually, it's the reverse! On a primary basis, we are always ruled by HaAlohim, since they are our archetypal parents. On special occasions, when our wickedness is very great, exceptions are granted where by which He allows certain of The Host of Heaven to rule over us; but even then, it is done in a very controlled manner by HaAlohim! Only those who are fully initiated into the holy mysteries understand these recondite spiritual matters.

Amongst these inferior Astrologers and Qabbalists, we again find the spurious equation between Shabbath and Saturn as Abenzra writes:

"*The fourth commandment concerning Shabbath corresponds to Saturn...*" (Commentary to Sefer Shmoth 20:14).

Now, it is an established fact amongst all the elite, wise, and veracious ancient Astrologers as seen in their books such as The Tetrabiblos, that every day of the week is associated with a planet. Hence, our most ancient and esoteric scroll states:

"*...7 planets in the Universe, 7 Days in the year...*" (Sefer Yetzirah 4:4).

And so the association between the 7 planets and 7 days. Now the correct enumeration and associations are also given in the scroll[12] supra as:

Day	1	2	3	4	5	6	7
Planet	Saturn	Jupiter	Mars	Sun	Venus	Mercury	Moon

And this is in accord with all of the most elite ancient Astrologers on record. Common sense dictating that this also represents the order of the spheres in terms of distance from the Earth. And to seal this Truth, I feel it is necessary to provide the scriptural proofs. For the sake of time, I will provide 5 of the 7 proofs. Let us begin, shall we?

Saturn rules over Day 1 as it is written:

---

[12] C.F. Ibid. 4:5-12 in the most ancient and veracious version of Sefer Yetzirah. There are a number of spurious versions, the GRA being one of them.

"*...and darkness was over the face of the abyss...Day One*" (Sefer Breyshith 1:1-5).

Ergo, darkness or blackness is associated with Day One. Furthermore, there are 4 main negative terms used: void, formless, darkness, and the abyss. Hence, Day 1 is associated with very negative or malefic attributes. From basic true Astrology we know Saturn is associated with the color black and that it is a malefic planet as it is written:

"*Saturn, when he gains sole dominance, is in general, the cause of destruction...*" (Tetrabiblos Book II Chapter 8 Of the Quality of the Predicted Event).

Mars rules over Day 3 as it is written:

"*...and let יבשה (the dry land) appear....third day.*" (Ibid. 1:9-13).

Day 3 is all about land appearing. And the Hebrew word יבשה also signifies 'dryness' and 'destruction'. Additionally, the Hebrew word אדמה (Adamah) which may also signify 'land', also signifies the color 'red'. These are all attributes associated with the planet Mars.

The Sun rules over Day 4 as it is written:

"*And Alohim made 2 great lights...the fourth day.*" (Ibid. 1:16-19).

The greatest light is the Sun, and so its association with the 4th Day. Additionally, the middle candlestick in the Menorah which was the biggest also signifies the Sun as evidenced by Philon Judaeus and Flavius Josephus:

"*For the Sun, like the candlestick, has the 4th place in the middle of the six...*" (Philo Judaeus Moses II 103).

Moreover, according to our esoteric mystical doctrines, TIFERETH who is the middle Emanation of the Lower 7 Sfiroth is symbolized by the Sun. These are all proofs within our theosophy and wisdom that the Sun rules over the 4th Day.

Venus rules over the 5th Day. In basic veracious Astrology, Venus is associated with fertility as it is written:

"*And Alohim blessed them saying, 'Increase and Multiply!'...the fifth day.*" (Ibid. 1:22-23).

The Moon is associated with Shabbath because in our esoteric telestic doctrines, these words are all code words or symbols for The Daughter of El who is SHEɧINAH as it is written:

"*Calculation of all is by the Moon....so here is the site of all equinoxes, solstices, intercalations, festivals, holidays, and Shabbaths.*

'Israel, cleaving to the Blessed Holy One count/calculate by the Moon.' (Talmud Babli Tractate Sukkah 29A)." (Sefer HaZohar 1:46B).

"*He made the Moon also to serve in her season for a declaration of times...From the Moon is the sign of Feasts (which include Shabbath!)...The month is called after her name.*" (LXX Yeshua Beyn Siraɧ).

And these the are seals proving that the 1st Day of the Month, New Moon, is determined by the Moon which then also determines Shabbath 7 days later! Q.E.D. for you ignorant Gentile Jesuits who may stumble upon this book.

And so now it should be readily seen that Saturn rules over Day 1 or the Holy Feast of New Moon and NOT Shabbath! For that is day of blackness and darkness as the Moon is completely blackened and dark. Mystery of the goat sacrifice for New Moon. For a malefic power rules over that day. And there are no goat sacrifices on Shabbath because it is entirely ruled by beneficent powers! Holy decrees cannot be broken!

The Bitten Olive

The Divine Lamb figures promimently in this Book of the Apocaplyse. Expansions and mysteries of only a few verses in HaTorah. The first telestic reference being found in:

"*And Abraham said: 'my son, Alohim will see Himself a lamb for a burnt offering...*" (Sefer Breyshith 22:8).

Now, this is the most common plain English Translation. This is not how we Qabbalists read it however, being more interested in the mystical layers of the text. The literal Hebrew, as we Qabbalists read, is:

"*And Abraham said: 'Alohim will see Himself a lamb for the burnt offering of my Son...*" (Ibid.).

In the original Hebrew, the word '*my Son*' comes at the end, NOT the beginning. This very mystically equates the 3 words – *lamb, burnt offering, and my Son.* To the Christian and initiated Jewish Qabbalist the references are clear. Morever, the Hebrew word for '*will see*' is evidently future tense. Mystically, this alludes to future deliverances through the Divine Lamb. Our ancient Sages mystically equate the blood of the Binding of Yitzaĥaq with the blood of Pesaĥ as it is written:

"*And I shall see the blood [of Pesaĥ] is I shall see the blood of the Binding of Yitzaĥaq as it is written:*

'*And Abraham called the name of this place:* יהוה *will see...' [Sefer Breyshith 22:14].*" (Meĥilta de Rab Yishmael 12:13).

The grand implications and ramifications of all this should easily be understood by the holy Initiate.

Now, as already explained in the commentary, 'lamb' is a codeword for a very high Divine Order, namely the Order of Malki-

Tzedeq. Principally it is headed by 2 Divine Lambs viz. the 2 Divine Serpents/Dragons. One is Mashiah, the other Lucifer as it is written:

"*And looking upon Yeshua as He walked, he saith, 'Behold the Lamb of Alohim'!*" (Sefer Yoḫanan 1:36).

"*And I beheld another Beast come up out of the Earth and he had 2 horns like a Lamb, and he spake as a Dragon.*" (Book of the Apocalypse 13:11).

Again, 'dragon' and 'lamb' are all codewords synonymous with the same Divine Order, ruled and run by the 2 same chief Alohim. Except, this Lamb is only a Lamb outwardly and not inwardly! The ancient esoteric seal/symbol of the Caduceus represents these 2 poles of this Divine Order. Each is the antithesis to the other.

Now there is grand Arcanum behind the most powerful corporate high magical ritual of Pesaḫ! And there are many mysteries surrounding it. To the vulgar Jew, the Egyptians worshipped the Constellation Aries and the lamb. And so now, the Christian is no different worshipping a lamb like them! Such gross oversimplicifations are the domain of the spiritually and intellectualy weak and inferior. Yet, what are we to say? The Pesaḫ sacrifice represented an indirect offering to this divine order, simultaneously neutralizing them, and yet it is to also represents the slaying of Mashiaḫ, offering divine protection??? At first glance, it doesn't seem to make sense! Yet this is precisely the quintessence of the holy mysteries, abound with divine paradoxes and antinomies!

There are 3 words for 'lamb' in ancient Hebrew, all alluding the very sublime nature of this divine order! These 3 words are: טלה כבש שה. כבש is of the aspect of GEBURAH, its spiritual source being in The Left Pillar. It's root meaning is 'to defeat', 'to opress', or 'to conquer'.

שה is a very special word. The root word is most obviously ש! Every letter of the Hebrew Alef-Beth is a divine seal. The letter ש is one of the more powerful seals representing EL SHADDAI. This seal is affixed to our mezuzoth. This seal is full of power and mysteries, one representing the unity of the supernal divine Trinity through its 3 prongs. Now, very interestingly we read in HaTorah:

"*שה (female lamb) תמים (plural perfect) male...*" ~ Sefer Shmoth 12:5

The word for 'lamb' in this verse is in the singular feminine. Yet, it is modified by a plural adjective – 'perfects', followed by a masculine modification! Oh, the mysticism and holy mysteries abound in HaTorah! Here we have a most high divine paradox or antinomy, namely the mystical equation of masculinity, singularity, femininity, and plurality in the Divine! And this is just one of numerous textual anomalies found in a kosher Scroll of HaTorah, all pointing to the higher holy mysteries.

This then makes the masculine Lamb – ש! Without the feminine suffix ה which represents His mate. Again, this is EL SHADDAI who is Metatron who is none other than HaMashiaḥ. The Gematria of this letter and seal is 300. Below are just some its equations.

הגורל ליהוה
The Lot of YHWH [Sefer Wayikra 16:8]

אריה מטה יהודה
The Lion of the Tribe of Yehudah

האל הגדול הגבורה
The Great Powerful El [Sefer Yermiyahu 32:18]

רוח אלהים
The Spirit of Alohim [Sefer Breyshith 1:2]

300 = 301 through Im Kollel. 301 is equal to אש (fire). And this is the great mystery of:

"*...He (Mashiaḥ) shall baptize you with the Holy Spirit and the Fire.*" (Sefer Mattityahu 3:11).

But let us return to the Divine Ewe, His mate, SHEḫINAH. The Gematria of שה is 305. This is equal to דשא (The Spring) and יצרה (The Female Form), all codewords for Her. Within this singular Mashiaḫ, a hermaphrodite, is found its mirror image! Behold, 305 is also equal to לרעה (The Evil) and ערלה (The Foreskin). Both words, very telestically, are permutations of each other! Both are symbols for Lucifer. Especially since it is the Archetypal Divine Matrix and Feminine who gave birth to him. For the 2 principal Alohim of the Lower Realms are the archetypal divine phalluses, one being circumcised, the other not. They are the 2 Trees, resembling phalluses, of the Garden of Eden. Vying for control of the Earth or Field, the archetypal divine Pudendum. Lastly, 305 = 306 though Im Kollel which is equal to אשה (The Woman). Everything is interconnected!

But allow me to take you even deeper into the Divne Well. The last remaining word is טלה. Sometimes it is also written as טלא. Now, the root meaning of this word is טל (dew) as it is written:

"…for my head is filled with טל …" (Shir HaShirim 5:2).

Again, telestically equating the Divine Lamb with the archetypal divine Phallus. Exoterically, it is written of this divine Dew:

"*All who occupy themselves with dew of HaTorah, the dew of HaTorah revives them.*" (Talmud Babli Tractate Ketuboth 111B).

Esoterically, it is written:

"*Behold, to thee is a symbol:*

'...my head is filled with dew...' [Shir HaShirim 5:2].

ה is SHEḫINAH in exile. Her completion and life is the טל (Dew with a Gematria of 39). And this is יוד הא ואו [1st 3 letters of Tetragrammaton fully spelled out with a Gematria of 39]. And ה is SHEḫINAH which is not from the Gematria of טל (Dew with a Gematria of 39). But:

יוד הא ואו *[1st 3 letters of Tetragrammaton fully spelled out with a Gematria of 39].*

This is equal to the Gematria of טל *(Dew with a Gematria of 39). Which fills SHEɧINAH from the flowing of all the supernal sources."*
Immediately, The Faithful Shepherd rose and the holy Patriarchs with him. Until here is the mystery of unity. From here on is the first section of the secrets of HaTorah." (Sefer Tiqquney HaZohar Tiqqun #7 17B).

When טל is affixed with ה, it is complete. The Gematria of טלה is 44 which is equal to 45 thorugh Im Kollel. This is equal to the Gematria of אדם (ADAM), ADAM Qadmon that is. And this is equal to the Gematria to the full expanision of the Holy Tetragrammaton!

יוד הא ואו הא [Tetragrammaton fully spelled out] (Combined Gematria of 45).

טלה is even more complete when it includes the letter א - טלאה. Who is א? Lo, it is written:

"*It has been taught in the Concealed Book, The Ancient of Ancients, Hidden of the Hidden, was arrayed and prepared, that is He existed and did not exist, did not actually exist yet was arrayed. No one knows Him, for He is more ancient than the ancients, but in his arrayal, He is known like an elder of elders...more concealed than the concealed – known by his signs yet unknown...Through 400,000 Universes the whiteness of Golgotha of his head spreads and from the radiance of this white, the saints inherit 400 Universes in the Universe that is coming...in Golgotha dwell 120 million Universes, moving with it, supported by it. From this Golgotha trickles* טל *(DEW) to the exterior one, filling his head everyday. And from that* טל *(DEW) , shaken from the head of the exterior one, the dead are awakened in the Universe that is Coming as it is written:*

'For my head is filled with dew...' [Shir HaShirim 5:2]." (Sefer HaZohar Idra Rabba 3:128B)

Golgotha is the name of the place where Mashiaĥ Bar Yosef was crucified. A great mystery that has never been understood by Christians for they were never fully initiated into the holy mysteries. It too is a codeword as now evinced. It is an occult reference to our Heavenly Great Grandfather who is KETHER. There are 3 Heads or Orders; or we may even say Phalluses. Mashiaĥ is the 3rd Order, an Image of The Image. And so hopefully, now, ye have tasted a little of the divine Dew of the Eternal Olive Tree!

Epilogue

The knowledge and wisdom presented here has been sealed for over 2000 years!!! And it is I, the Chief Magician of Mystery Babylon, a son of King Dawid of Beth Dawid that has revealed it here for the first time! I could have easily said and added so much more! But this is enough for now.

May it spread the knowledge and wisdom of the kingdom of יהוה. May the LOVE of Adoneinu YESHUAH bar (pun intended) יהוה HaMashiaḫ be with ye all. Mara Atha (The LORD Cometh) Amen.

ת

THE END

www.ingramcontent.com/pod-product-compliance
Lightning Source LLC
Chambersburg PA
CBHW021408290426
44108CB00010B/442
9780692959145